Rock and Roll Doctor

Lowell George: guitarist, songwriter,
and founder of **Little Feat**

Rock and Roll Doctor

Lowell George: guitarist, songwriter, and founder of **Little Feat**

MARK BREND

Backbeat Books

Rock and Roll Doctor

Lowell George: guitarist, songwriter, and founder of **Little Feat**
by Mark Brend

A BACKBEAT BOOK
First edition 2002
Published by Backbeat Books
600 Harrison Street,
San Francisco, CA 94107
www.backbeatbooks.com

An imprint of The Music Player Network United
Entertainment Media Inc.

Published for Backbeat Books by Outline Press Ltd,
115J Cleveland Street, London W1T 6PU, England.
www.backbeatuk.com

ISBN 0-87930-726-9

Art Director: Nigel Osborne
Design: Paul Cooper
Editor: Tony Bacon
Production: Phil Richardson

Printed by Colorprint (Hong Kong)

02 03 04 04 06 5 4 3 2 1

Contents

I Wish You Knew
The Story

"There was nothing regular about the guy."

ELIZABETH GEORGE DESCRIBES HER HUSBAND, LOWELL

Take a casual glance through a selection of albums by Californian rock acts from the 1970s and you'll see an apparently interchangeable host of Laurel Canyon desperados, cosmic cowboys and jet-set drifters. There was an identifiable type, men and women sharing a studied laidback look: bronzed, denim-clad and long-haired.

Musically there were shared features too. Harmonies were high and slick and the favoured groove was mid-paced and easygoing. Record-company rosters were full of carefully packaged outlaws peddling the myth of an elusive nirvana somewhere between rock'n'roll excess and the easy sunshine life. It was an alluring notion, but one that proved to be as illusory as the previous decade's dreams of an earthly paradise. In the middle of this world was Lowell George. He too appeared laidback, was often denim clad, and wore his hair long. But he was also portly, mildly dishevelled, and had a calm, beatific expression. He was like a crumpled guru. And while his music had those mid-paced grooves and high

School photograph of a teenage Lowell George

harmonies, there was something rough and ready about it. Danny Hutton of Three Dog Night puts it this way: "Lowell George was part of the Californian thing, sure, but he was a lot more soulful. He was a hybrid: country, but way on the funky side."[1]

George was a regular face on the party and studio circuit, yet somehow he always looked askance on the scene, quizzical and ironic. He was present without ever really belonging, both a committed participant and a wry observer, a leading light and an elusive background presence. According to his friend Martin Kibbee, "Lowell was the best-kept secret of the 1970s mellow mafia."[2] He was a true rock'n'roll original.

FAMILY LIFE ON MULHOLLAND DRIVE

Fittingly, the man Jackson Browne called "the Orson Welles of rock'n'roll" spent his early life on the fringes of Hollywood movie society. Lowell George was born shortly before the end of World War II, on April 13th 1945. His father, Willard George, was a furrier to the Hollywood stars of the 1930s and '40s and was said to be friendly with WC Fields, among others. George Snr had been successful in his trade and was able to build a house for his family on Mulholland Drive, between Laurel Canyon Boulevard and Woodrow Wilson Drive. It was in this comfortable environment that George spent his early years, along with his father, his mother Florence, and a brother, Hampton, who was five years older. Errol Flynn was a neighbour, and in later years George liked to tell a story about Flynn's pet monkey coming into their garden and stealing an apple from the young Lowell's hand. When Willard George died in the mid 1950s, Florence remarried and the family moved to Outpost Drive, a little further along Mulholland toward Hollywood.

Both Willard and Florence George were creative. Florence in particular was artistically inclined, and she played the piano. It was against this backdrop that George's interest in music first became apparent, very early in his life. It was an interest that was to blossom into a lifelong passion. His first musical instrument was the harmonica which he started to learn when he was about five years old. The young George took lessons but was a somewhat recalcitrant pupil, preferring to play by ear rather than learn to sight-read. His first public performance of note was with his brother on a TV talent show where the two performed a harmonica duet. Around the time of that brief early moment of showbusiness glory George met his lifetime friend and collaborator, Martin Kibbee. The two were pupils at North Hollywood Junior High. From there they moved to Hollywood High School where other pupils included Lowell's future wife Elizabeth, and Paul Barrère, who later became second guitarist in Little Feat.

At high school George played the flute in the marching band and school orchestra. He was, according to his friend Van Dyke Parks among others, a fine flautist. It is said that he chose the instrument because it was light and therefore didn't require much effort to carry during marching-band processions. It was while learning the flute that he also finally got the hang of sight-reading. Kibbee recalls, "On one occasion at orchestra practice he turned the sheet music upside down and then played his upside-down part so convincingly that the rest of the band stopped playing in astonishment."[3] George eventually abandoned the flute as his main instrument. He believed that Roland Kirk had already taken it to its limits.

By this time George was also playing guitar. He had started at the age of 11 when he took over his brother's classical guitar while Hampton was away serving in the armed forces. Lowell then quickly graduated to a Fender Mustang guitar and Fender Champ amplifier, a typical beginner's electric-guitar package of the time. With this set-up he embarked on the time-honoured adolescent pursuit of playing too loud and annoying his mother. Later, he moved up-scale to Fender Stratocasters, and then experimented with Gibson ES-335s among others. He would eventually return to the Stratocaster, and it is that guitar with which he is most readily associated.

Apart from the guitar, flute and harmonica, George also learned to play saxophone, sitar and shakuhachi (a Japanese flute-like instrument). Over the course of his life his musical tastes ranged far and wide, encompassing rock, jazz, South American folk, country, modern classical, and much else. His wife Elizabeth says he would sometimes go into a record shop and speculatively purchase half a dozen records about which he knew little, just to find out what they sounded like.[4]

As a teenager and aspiring bohemian, George's main musical interest was jazz. He said, "I hated rock'n'roll then. At that point it was the Frankie Avalon story ... who wanted it? Who needed it?"[5] Kibbee backs this up, saying, "His taste in music at that time ran more to West Coast jazz than, say, Jan & Dean or The Beach Boys. Les McCann and Mose Allison were appearing at Sunset Strip clubs like The Bit and The Renaissance where we hung out. Lowell wore a black turtleneck, the whole beatnik bit: Maynard G Krebs looking for Tuesday Weld in *The Many Loves Of Dobie Gillis*."[6]

After Hollywood High, George left home and went to Valley Junior College to study art and art history. He stayed for a couple of years but did not graduate. While studying he worked briefly in a gas station to support himself, an experience he later credited as the inspiration for his early truck-driving songs 'Willin'' and 'Truck Stop Girl'.

Being curious by temperament, he had a wide range of interests apart from music. He was a martial arts practitioner and, according to some claims, was a karate black belt. He had a great fascination for World War II aeroplanes and became knowledgeable about them. His other hobbies included fishing and building remote-controlled model aeroplanes and rockets.

George's adult family life was complicated. He spent most of the 1970s (from about 1971) with Elizabeth George. They were married in 1976. George had two sons, Forrest and Luke, from a previous marriage. Elizabeth also had a son, Jedadiah (Jed), from an earlier marriage. The couple's family was completed by the arrival of a daughter in 1974. George's rock'n'roll lifestyle and obsessive working habits may have sometimes caused tensions at home, but despite this George was always a warm family man and a devoted father.

Elizabeth George provides a touching vignette of their family life around the time that Little Feat were working on their fourth album, *Feats Don't Fail Me Now*, in 1974 (see chapter 6). She was heavily pregnant when Little Feat went to Maryland to record the album. The George family – Lowell, Elizabeth, Luke, Jed and Forrest – moved en masse, driving across the country to a rented house in a rural area near the studio. Here, Elizabeth recalls, Lowell was the hero of the neighbourhood children thanks to the model rockets he launched from time to time.[7] She eventually went into labour there when George had briefly returned to Hollywood for a performance with the band. He flew back and met his wife at the hospital in time for the birth of their daughter, Inara George. Inara's middle name is Maryland – the choice of her father. While this was going on, Little Feat engineer George Massenburg and his wife were babysitting the three boys. The next day George, despite having had no sleep, took the boys fishing.

LOWELL'S SENSE OF HUMOUR

George's speaking voice was generally quiet and measured. He had a fondness for multi-syllabic words, and these would find their way into his conversation and song lyrics. His facility with language and his soft voice were particularly effective tools for expressing his oblique, droll humour. People who were close to George invariably comment on this sense of humour when remembering him, using words like abstract and surreal to describe it.

A friend, Ira Ingber, tells a story that gives a flavour of this appealing characteristic. "He once showed up to a birthday party for me," Ingber recalls, "and entered the room with a finely-crafted pine box. Wordlessly, he slowly opened the box, revealing a pair of perfectly chromed, full-size motorcycle boots. He allowed the room to ooh and ah, and then closed the box. He then exited, saying nothing."[8]

George's humour found its way into many of his best songs and can also be detected in the dry remarks that season his interviews with journalists. He had the gift of being able to share an irony with an audience, as if the twinkle in his eye could be discerned across a darkened auditorium or be seen glinting from the grooves of a record. It was a big part of his appeal.

Lowell George died in 1979 at the age of 34. For the previous 13 years or so he had been pursuing a career in music, having decided in his late teens that there was more to rock'n'roll than Frankie Avalon. After all, by then it was the era of The Beatles, The Byrds, The Rolling Stones, Bob Dylan, and the burgeoning hippie movement. *Rolling Stone* magazine wrote in George's obituary that when he saw The Byrds perform at the Brave New World coffeehouse it had marked a pivotal moment in his conversion.

At the age of 20 George had come into some family money. He abandoned his art studies and formed his first band, The Factory, with Kibbee. After that, around late 1967 and early '68, he briefly returned to college, studying music theory. He also studied sitar for a while with Ravi Shankar. But by now he was steadily walking the rock'n'roll path and these episodes were temporary diversions, even if informative and useful. There followed brief spells with The Standells and The Mothers Of Invention before George formed Little Feat with Bill Payne. The two would share good times and bad during that band's peculiar, uneven and vibrant life through the 1970s.

There was much about George's career that was typical for a rock musician of his generation. There was the garage-band apprenticeship, the discovery of the recording studio as a creative playpen, the long tours, the squabbles with other band members. There were the undulating fortunes abruptly cut off by an early death. Yet for all that it remains a career that is hard to categorise, just as he was a man who was hard to categorise. As Elizabeth George says, "There was nothing regular about the guy."[9]

If the value of a musician can be measured by the respect of his or her peers then Lowell George was a true great. Bonnie Raitt said, "He was the best singer, songwriter and guitar player I have ever heard, hands down, in my life."[10] There are many who would say something similar, including estimable talents such as Van Dyke Parks, John Sebastian from The Lovin' Spoonful, Danny Hutton from Three Dog Night, Jackson Browne, and a host of others, well-known names as well as obscure background figures.

Lowell George was hard working, driven and prolific, obsessed with making music. The music he made – with Little Feat, as a solo artist, and as a session player and collaborator – was rich, fertile, varied, erratic, sometimes frustrating, and shot through with inspiration and humour. He liked to describe his songs as "cracked mosaics". This book is about the glinting fragments that make up those cracked mosaics, and how they were stuck together. It is about the music of Lowell George, and how it was made.

CHAPTER 2

The Lightning-Rod Man

> "I don't know what Lowell learned from Frank Zappa, but if it was the same as the rest of us, he learned a lot about music."

JIMMY CARL BLACK, MOTHERS OF INVENTION

In the mid 1960s the United States was teeming with newly formed young bands. It was just like a decade before when the first generation of rock'n'roll stars emerged, with new musical possibilities inspiring a host of imitators, originators and bandwagon jumpers. There were two dominant schools of inspiration: the British Invasion, led by The Beatles and The Rolling Stones alongside less credible names from the period like Herman's Hermits, and the new folk-rock hybrid spearheaded by The Byrds. But there was much more going on besides.

Bob Dylan's new abstract electric poetry was endearing him to rock audiences just as it distanced him from the folk establishment. The Motown and Stax labels began turning out a rich stream of soul singles that crossed effortlessly into the pop charts. Under Brian Wilson's guidance, The Beach Boys

Lowell (far left) in The Mothers Of Invention, next to future Feat member Roy Estrada

were evolving from the innocence of the pre-Beatles surf scene into innovative pop giants. The first shoots of the hippy counter-culture were springing up in a season of psychedelic experimentation amid a dissatisfaction with dominant conservative values.

It was against this backdrop that countless young Americans grouped together in garages, plugged their Fender Mustang guitars into Vox amplifiers, and ripped through 'Hey Joe' and 'Louie, Louie'. "Garage punk" as it now called is in fact a convenient holdall for a whole spectrum of American acts of the period. Most of these so-called garage bands were musical primitives with more enthusiasm than dexterity, destined to play their local circuit for a while and maybe record a demo that would appear on a collectors' compilation decades later, dubbed from a scratchy acetate. Others left their garages way behind and went much further with their careers, cutting records, touring, even having hits. Delving back through the early days of American musicians who were later to rise to prominence in the 1970s, you find that this was the musical nursery in which many cut their teeth.

It isn't a surprise, then, to find that Lowell George was no exception, and that he served a significant part of his musical apprenticeship in two garage bands of the period. In fact those bands were too competent and too professional to deserve the label, but for better or worse that is how they are now seen by the people who recall them. Both were Los Angeles bands and both were stamped with a number of the characteristics of some of the big acts that flourished in what by then was the biggest music-producing city in the United States.

GARAGE AND THE LOS ANGELES MUSIC SCENE

Like many cities and towns in America between 1965 and 1968, the vast urban sprawl of Los Angeles and surrounding districts spawned hundreds, even thousands, of garage bands, almost all now long lost to everyone but the most devoted enthusiasts. More importantly, though, it hosted a rich, fertile mainstream rock scene, dominated by bands now recognised as among the best and most influential of the era. The Beach Boys were thriving, virtually the only American band to flourish through and beyond the British Invasion. But by 1965 they were already international stars and seemed in a sense separate from any local scene. The Byrds, however, remained a dominant local force despite international success. Having initiated a brief folk-rock craze in 1965 with their classic electric rendition of Dylan's 'Mr Tambourine Man' they built on early achievements by virtue of constant experimentation and development.

Other scene-leaders were Love, led by Arthur Lee, and The Seeds. Slightly later came Buffalo Springfield, and a little later still The Doors. Love evolved from punkish folk-rock to the acoustic majesty of their *Forever Changes* album in a few short years. The Seeds were a lesser name, but regulars on the circuit as well. Essentially a garage band made good, they were musically limited, but a big live draw thanks to the antics of their eccentric frontman, Sky Saxon. They had a penchant for recycling the two-chord riff from their 1965 hit single 'Pushin Too Hard'. Some reports suggest that Lowell George joined the Seeds briefly, but there is no documentary or recorded evidence for this, and most of George's contemporaries have no recollection of such a liaison. He did share bills with The Seeds, though, as he led his first band around the labyrinthine netherworld of clubs on the Los Angeles underground scene. And the shadows of The Seeds, of The Byrds and of Love are cast over the surviving recorded legacy of George's first band.

Pictures of The Factory show the youthful, already chubby face of George framed by a typical pudding-basin or cereal-bowl haircut of the period, gazing out inscrutably across the years. Partly as a result of George's reluctance to give away too much information about his early work, and partly as a result of their low-profile career, information about The Factory is scant.

Their story started some time in late 1965 or early 1966. A nucleus of George, by then a 20-year-old novice bohemian, his old schoolfriend Martin Kibbee on bass, and guitarist Warren Klein came together and started to scout around for a drummer. George was the singer and also played rhythm guitar and woodwind instruments, primarily flute. He wrote most of the band's material, sometimes sharing credits with Kibbee or Klein. George's friend Ira Ingber (brother of Captain Beefheart guitarist Elliot Ingber) watched the embryonic Factory rehearse, and remembers that George "seemed to be the first among equals".[1] According to Kibbee the band was launched with $10,000 of family money when both he and George "cashed in our grandfathers' stock, bought a van, amps, electric guitars, and basically never stopped working".[2] They lived together in a house in the Hollywood Hills where they spent much of their time rehearsing.

The Factory's initial drummer was one Cary Slavin. The sequence of events when he left (to join the Moonies, according to Kibbee) are variously remembered by the interested parties – and among those memories is a recurring one that involves Dallas Taylor, later the drummer with Crosby Stills Nash & Young.

According to George,[3] Taylor was playing with The Factory following an appendix operation. During the show his wound opened and he started to bleed heavily. In considerable discomfort, Taylor's drumming deteriorated, but he continued playing without explaining what was happening as he was keen to keep the job because he needed the money. Drummer Richie Hayward, new in town from Ames, Iowa, and looking for work, was watching in the audience. He approached George afterwards, volunteering himself to replace the seemingly inadequate Taylor, and George agreed, only discovering Taylor's plight many years later. Another version of the story has Hayward responding to an advertisement after the unfortunate Taylor was dismissed following the post-operative incident.[4] The ad in question was placed in *The Los Angeles Free Press*: "Drummer Wanted. Must Be Freaky."

Hayward took up occupancy as The Factory's drummer after an intimidating audition at the band's pad, surrounded by various members of Frank Zappa's Mothers Of Invention. Whatever really happened, by late 1966 Hayward was drumming for The Factory.

The arrival of Hayward in The Factory alongside George marked the beginning of an important musical relationship. In late 1969, after the demise of the group, Hayward would join George again, this time in the first line-up of Little Feat. Today, he continues to drum for the current incarnation of the band. Another Factory member, Martin Kibbee, would also feature in George's later career. Under the pen name Fred Martin he would co-write several Little Feat standards with George, including 'Dixie Chicken' and 'Rock And Roll Doctor'.

Apart from George's involvement, The Factory's career was unremarkable, although the band did show enough promise to be self-supporting after the initial cash injection. They also managed two television appearances, firstly appearing as The Bedbugs in an episode of *F-Troop* (1967), a sitcom set in the time of the old West, in which George has a couple of small speaking lines, and then the same year as a contemporary bar band in another show, *Gomer Pyle*, performing two songs, 'Lost' and 'Candy Cane Madness', while Gomer Pyle himself looks for his date in a club.

Despite this exposure, The Factory remained just one of many bands doing the rounds and looking for a break – although legend has them distinguished from their many contemporaries by virtue of playing 'Hey Joe' louder than any other Los Angeles band at the time. But careful attention to what has survived of the band's music reveals dimensions that raise them above typical garage bands of the era and that hint at future glories.

THE FACTORY, ON RECORD

For 25 years The Factory's available recorded legacy was limited to one or two very obscure singles released on the UNI label, and a track recorded with Frank Zappa, 'Lightning-Rod Man', that became known through various appearances on bootlegs. That changed when those recordings, along with several other demos and outtakes, appeared on a 1993 collection entitled *Lightning-Rod Man*, credited to Lowell George And The Factory. (See discography at the back of this book.) The CD is dominated by tracks from two sources, one a set of recordings made for UNI, the other an audition tape for Herb Cohen, then Frank Zappa's manager. Additionally the collection features two songs produced by Zappa himself, and four songs recorded for Herb Cohen during the period between the demise of The Factory and the emergence of Little Feat. From our point of view these last songs are misplaced on the album, not being strictly a part of The Factory story, and so are dealt with in later chapters.

The six UNI cuts date from early 1966 to the summer of 1967. They were all produced by Marshall Leib, who had once been a member of Phil Spector's band The Teddy Bears. Emil Richards contributes various exotic percussion instruments to some of the recordings. Several of the songs are clearly indebted to The Byrds, the best of these being 'Candy Cane Madness' (written by George/Klein) with its harmony vocal and descending 12-string guitar patterns. 'Smile, Let Your Life Begin' (George) is more original, a cheery pop tune built on a military marching-beat foundation provided by Hayward and noted session drummer Earl Palmer. George plays piccolo and Richards cymbalum (small cymbals or bells), adding novel textures to a song listed as the b-side to the band's first UNI single, 'When I Was An Apple'. 'No Place I'd Rather Be' (George/Klein) is the song sometimes listed as the band's second single for UNI. It was recorded in 1967, the so-called summer of love, and features suitable lyrics about the "sun cascading to the ground". Richards's water chimes and Klein's heavily reverb'd raga guitar add yet more period detail.

The three songs that The Factory recorded for Herb Cohen and Zappa date from relatively early in the band's life (August 8th 1966) when Cary Slavin was still playing drums. They reveal a more primitive sound, very reminiscent of the high-octane folk-rock of the first Love album, with a dash of The Seeds' punk attitude.

It is no surprise that the two songs credited as Frank Zappa productions, 'Lightning-Rod Man' and 'The Loved One' (both George/Kibbee), tend toward a more experimental style than the other Factory material available. 'The Loved One' is mildly eerie mid-paced folk-rock featuring Kibbee's fuzz bass and Zappa on prepared piano. 'Lightning-Rod Man', based on a Herman Melville short story about a man who sells lightning conductors in thunderstorms, is unlike anything else the band recorded. Largely on account of George's barking vocal, the song bears such a strong resemblance to early Captain Beefheart recordings that it was sometimes later mistakenly identified as a Beefheart outtake.

And that's the only recorded evidence left of George's first band, The Factory. They were derivative, certainly, and very much of their time, but they were a lot more than a garage band. Maybe they did play 'Hey Joe' louder than anyone else, but they also experimented with water chimes, piccolo and prepared piano, and wrote songs based on literary works by great American writers. In The Factory's brief recorded legacy there are hints of later eclecticism, intelligence and experimentation, even if buried under period detail and hurried along by the enthusiasm of youth. And just as some of George's later musical journeys are first hinted at in a number of Factory recordings, so are other aspects of his character that shaped his later career. Kibbee says that George's controlling tendency, what he describes as one of Frank's laws ("I'm the leader and you guys play what I tell ya"[5]), came from the band's experience of working with Zappa. Similarly, George's later mistrust of the business side of music – which led him to form his own publishing company with Kibbee in the early 1970s – had its origins in The Factory's unproductive liaison with UNI Records.

LOWELL JOINS THE STANDELLS

Martin Kibbee, Richie Hayward and Warren Klein immediately found new employment when The Factory closed down in late 1967 or early 1968. They formed The Fraternity Of Man, a group now remembered for contributing 'Don't Bogart Me' to the *Easy Rider* soundtrack. That left Lowell George, by now an accomplished multi-instrumentalist and singer, casting around for something to do. For a while he filled his time attending college in Los Angeles, studying music theory. When John Fleck, an old friend from Hollywood High School, offered him the chance to join The Standells, George took it willingly enough. He was later to imply that this decision was driven more by the fact that he had nothing else to do rather than as a calculated career move. Whether it was a step forward or a step backward is open to question. Compared to The Factory, The Standells were big news commercially. Or at least they had been, a few years before. Musically, though, they were if anything more conservative. But whatever the direction this new step took George, it was apparently taken casually and without commitment.

The Standells had formed in Los Angeles in 1962 and spent a busy but unremarkable first four years of their career recording for Liberty, MGM and Vee Jay. They were also television regulars, a guest appearance on *The Munsters* being their best-remembered small-screen appearance. But the band looked set to be just one of many competent, hard-working West Coast bands … until in 1966 they fell in with producer, manager and songwriter Ed Cobb.

Cobb persuaded an initially reluctant band to record his song 'Dirty Water' and The Standells found themselves with a big hit, the song reaching number 11 in 1966. 'Dirty Water' is a classic garage-rock concoction. It is built around an irresistible riff played on both organ and lead guitar over which mildly anti-establishment sentiments are snarled in a voice typical of the cross-cultural exchange common at the time – white American copying Jagger copying black American bluesman. While The Standells never reached such commercial heights again, a tour with the Stones, four albums, and a succession of strong singles based on the 'Dirty Water' template saw them maintain a reasonable profile through 1966 and 1967. But by 1968 the times had changed. A new generation of bands with longer hair and longer guitar solos were emerging all down the West Coast. The Standells looked and sounded dated. Their drummer and main vocalist Dick Dodd left early in 1968, leaving founder members guitarist Tony Valentino and organist Larry Tamblyn (brother of film actor Russ Tamblyn) to patch together a new line-up of The Standells in an attempt to restore failing fortunes. A now forgotten drummer was recruited, and John Fleck was brought in to occupy the oft-vacated position of bass player. He in turn introduced George to The Standells. Speaking some years later, George simply said: "[Fleck] called me up and I auditioned, and they liked the way I sang so I got the job."[6]

George shared lead vocals with Tamblyn, and also played guitar and sitar. He was charged with singing many of the songs that had previously been handled by Dodds, the erstwhile frontman, drummer and lead vocalist, something that was to cause George some consternation. Because The Standells had been a briefly popular chart act they still had the vestiges of a female following during George's time in the band, a following which was focused mainly on the darkly handsome Dodds. As a sex object the already portly George was no replacement for the departed drummer and was not warmly received by some of the band's audience.

George said: "All these young girls [that Dodds] had gathered as an audience came looking for me after a gig one night to do me in. They thought I was responsible for his demise ... [and] I was in fear for my life for the next four gigs, because these girls kept showing up [who] weren't averse to carrying razor-blades in their coiffures."[7]

George's spell with The Standells was to be a brief one, lasting no more than six to eight weeks around early summer to late October or early November 1968, before he joined The Mothers Of Invention. According to organist Tamblyn, George played just a handful of dates with The Standells. "The only one I remember," he says, "was at Pierce College in Canoga Park, California. It was an afternoon concert, outdoors. As part of the show, Lowell sat on the floor and played the sitar and sang. It was quite a departure from the group's sound."[8]

The sitar was briefly popular as a rock instrument in the late 1960s after pioneering use first by George Harrison and later Brian Jones. Master Indian sitar player Ravi Shankar was also popular among the rock audience thanks to festival appearances and the endorsement of The Beatles. Shankar was living in Los Angeles at the time, and Lowell George later made reference to studying Indian music under Shankar for a year. The extent and exact nature of this tuition and how far George went with his studies is hard to quantify, but Tamblyn remembers that George did appear to have some formal knowledge of the instrument. "When he played the instrument, it was in the East Indian fashion, sitting lotus on the floor, bare-footed. I also remember he was a very good sitarist."[9] Elizabeth George, whom Lowell married in 1976, recalls: "Whenever he got involved in something he got completely involved. [George and Shankar] knew each other quite well and Ravi was very supportive of Lowell. It was all about learning different aspects of music."[10]

Although Tamblyn remembers George as a "pretty decent fellow", it wasn't long before relationships between him and the rest of the band deteriorated. George's sitar was, indirectly, the catalyst for this. Tamblyn remembers travelling to a particular concert in George's VW bus. "Lowell was driving. I was in the back seat with three other members of the group and Lowell's sitar, which he propped up on the seat back. Going around a curve, I accidentally leaned on the sitar, and the gourd [body] broke completely off. Even though I apologised, I think that began our adversarial relationship."[11] That sitar must have been replaced or repaired, though, because Elizabeth George recalls that he eventually sold his sitar to future Little Feat member Fred Tackett, and that it was destroyed in a fire when Tackett's house burned down.

When in the 1970s George talked of The Standells he adopted a tone somewhere between good-humoured irony and casual contempt. In an interview with *Zigzag* he spoke little about musical matters in relation to the band, instead making fun of other members taking hairdryers on the road. (Incidentally, the tape of the interview from which those quotes were drawn is punctuated by a voice persistently reminding George that he is late for his "hair appointment".[12])

Although this brief phase in his apprenticeship was musically unproductive and had little bearing on later events, it did again reveal a desire to control the musicians he was working with. This was a tendency that was to surface throughout his career, with a variety of results. Tamblyn says: "Lowell really had a need to be in total control. But when he insisted we grease back our hair and become a fifties band, Lowell and The Standells parted company. I think it was because of the low esteem in which he held the other members of the group – he felt we were beneath anything other than a fifties parody. We were nothing more than a bunch of rock'n'rollers. After all, none of us had studied with Ravi Shankar."[13]

Something else that George learned from The Standells was that bands were vulnerable to financial exploitation. Although not a really big name, and well past their peak, the group were still capable of earning reasonable money from concerts during George's time in the ranks. He was later to note how little of this money seemed to come to the band. So here was another factor that helped breed in him a cynicism about the workings of the music business and a degree of canniness when he later became more involved in managing his own affairs.

No known record of George's brief, ill-starred stint in The Standells survives, neither a recording nor a photograph. Tantalisingly, though, The Standells with George did make a band-funded recording of one of George's songs. Tamblyn says: "It was so different from The Standells' sound that no record company was interested in it. I can't remember the title. Lowell wrote and sang it, and as far as I know no copies of it exist."[14]

LOWELL GEORGE AND THE MOTHERS OF INVENTION

If George's decision to throw in his lot briefly with this once-great band now in terminal decline was slightly puzzling, then his next move was altogether more understandable. With their debut album, the 1966 double-LP *Freak Out*, The Mothers Of Invention had set new standards for challenging and sometimes complex art-rock (although of course it wasn't called that then). Under the dogmatic, visionary and dictatorial leadership of Frank Zappa, who was described by *Rolling Stone* as "a supreme genius of American music today",[15] they had been prolifically recording and touring their curious crossover of high-art and trash to no great chart success. But they were at least making a living, and were a more than credible creative force.

Zappa himself was an unusual man. With his long hair and drooping moustache he looked as dangerously odd as any rock musician then active. His recordings, too, were often scatological in the extreme. Yet in spite of this he was in some respects a conservative and conventional man, opposed to drug use, well organised, and an astute enough businessman to keep more control of his songs and recordings than was then normal for an artist. He also had a strong work ethic that he communicated forcefully to the musicians he hired.

Zappa and George had encountered each other before, both appearing as children on a particular television show (either the *Al Jarvis Amateur Hour* or *Arthur Godfrey Television Show* – accounts differ). Zappa put on a puppet show; George played a musical duet with his brother. Some reports have the George brothers winning the contest; others have both them and Zappa losing to a girl who tapdanced.

According to Mothers Of Invention drummer Jimmy Carl Black, "Lowell was originally hired by Frank to sing lead. Ray Collins [the previous Mothers' singer] had quit again and we had no vocalist."[16] George would have joined with no illusions that his new role as lead vocalist would have the stature and significance attached to it that it does in most other groups. Zappa's band members, even his frontmen, were very much hired hands who were there to help him substantiate his own idiosyncratic vision. Additionally, George felt that Collins had contributed something to the Mothers that he couldn't possibly replicate. "No one can replace Ray," George recalled a little later.

"He's a singer par excellence and has a sense of humour that I couldn't hope to get near. I wound up playing more guitar than singing."[17] So although the new job was not quite as prestigious as it might have seemed at first glance, it did prove a good professional move. George earned a living from the Mothers for a while and, more importantly, he learned a great deal from Zappa. And through his association with the Mothers he would come across three people who would soon loom large in the story of Little Feat – Roy Estrada, Billy Payne, and Neon Park.

Such is the continuing interest in Zappa that his career is still researched, documented and discussed in great depth. This makes it relatively easy to determine with some accuracy when George served with the Mothers. According to Zappa enthusiast Charles Ulrich, George's first gig with The Mothers Of Invention almost certainly took place on November 8th 1968 in Fullerton, California. What seem to be his guitar playing and singing are audible on a tape of that show. Furthermore, Zappa referred to Lowell George and Buzz Gardner as the two newest members of his band in a radio broadcast on November 27th. Allowing for the likelihood of a week or two in which to rehearse and generally settle in, George probably joined the Mothers in late October or early November of 1968.

Ulrich also says that George's last confirmed gig with the Mothers was on May 23rd 1969 in Appleton, Wisconsin. There may have been another gig in Toronto the following day, in which case Lowell was presumably still in the band. But it seems certain he did not go on the European tour of May-June 1969.[18] These dates concur with Jimmy Carl Black's recollection that George was with the Mothers for six or seven months, and that he left the band "just before we went to England for the 1969 tour".[19]

It is more difficult, however, to tell which Mothers Of Invention recordings George contributed to. The picture is muddied by the fact that their album sleeves of the period sometimes pictured and credited the current band at the time of release, whether or not that matched the personnel heard on the album. Given the fluidity of the line-up and the number of releases – seven Mothers and Zappa albums between 1966 and 1969 – this causes some confusion. For example, George's name appears on the cover and his photograph appears in a booklet for the 1968 double-LP *Uncle Meat*, although he joined the band after the album was recorded.

It is clear that George appeared on *Weasels Ripped My Flesh*, a collection of outtakes recorded by various Mothers line-ups between 1967 and 1969, released in 1970. He is credited as rhythm guitarist and vocalist on the first track 'Didja Get Any Onya?' and probably plays on several other songs. 'Didja' is a free-form jazz work-out relying heavily on squawking horns and muttered, overlaid vocals, recorded live at the Philadelphia Arena. It is one of the most experimental commercially-available recordings that George was involved in during his entire career. He is also thought to have contributed to 1969's *Burnt Weeny Sandwich*. Various George contributions also appear on the retrospective series *You Can' t Do That On Stage Anymore* that first appeared in the late 1980s (see discography).

George himself started a long-running discussion by claiming in David Walley's 1972 book, *No Commercial Potential*, that he appeared on Zappa's 1969 solo album, *Hot Rats*. If that is the case, there are no obvious George trademarks to reveal his presence. There is no slide guitar, and the one vocal performance, 'Willie The Pimp', was taken by Captain Beefheart. Furthermore, some Zappa historians[20] record that Zappa started laying down tracks for this album in August 1969, in other words after George had left the Mothers. One possibility is that George worked on early versions of the material that eventually appeared on *Hot Rats*. Zappa was well known for re-working material, a tendency he called "a life of progressive overdubbage".[21]

If George was involved in the recording of *Hot Rats* then his contribution was almost certainly minor. In fact, George's musical contribution to the Mothers and Zappa's solo work during that period from late 1968 to mid 1969 is of no real consequence, as he himself agreed. "I was really performing no function in the band,"[22] he said later. Nonetheless George's spell with Zappa was important, if only for what he learned. As Black says, "I don't know what Lowell learned from Frank, but if it was the same as the rest of us, he learned a lot about music."[23] That is true – but he learned other things as well.

LEARNING FROM FRANK ZAPPA

As we have already seen, George's controlling tendencies as a musician had surfaced – and caused tensions – in both The Factory and The Standells. There was no chance to do the same in The Mothers Of Invention, something that George seemed to have accepted from the start. As Black says, "Frank was the boss of the Mothers, period. At the time Lowell was in the Mothers he was a fairly young man and was just happy to be playing with us. Frank had very specific things he wanted from everyone in the band. And he got them."[24]

But if George knew he was never going to have influence in the Mothers, he was able to learn something about Zappa's style of leading a band. Essentially, this involved choosing great musicians, and then guiding them very clearly in what they should do. George saw in Zappa's management of the Mothers a model of how a band could be run. It was a model that worked, that was productive, and that allowed for individual creativity – but within the clear boundaries set by the bandleader. This idea of how things might be was to stay with him throughout his career.

What else did Lowell George learn from his few months playing with Frank Zappa? Many traces of Zappa's influence crop up later in his career. Perhaps not direct and obvious influences, but certainly attitudes, ways of thinking, methods for doing things. It would be wrong to suggest that George learned all of these things directly from Zappa only, or even that Zappa was a very powerful factor in George's development. Perhaps it is more the case that George saw in Zappa a successful, productive application of many of his own nascent interests, obsessions and tendencies.

A few years after leaving the Mothers, George would immerse himself in studio work. He said, "I write tunes and use tape like someone would use manuscript paper. To me it's the same thing. It's like tools to me: a tape recorder is like a pencil and tape is like paper."[25] Zappa was much the same. Like all rock bands of the time, The Mothers Of Invention played live regularly. But it was in the recording studio that Zappa established his kingdom. Ever since he set up his own Studio Z earlier in the decade Zappa had embarked on a regular recording routine of 12-hour days, generating miles of tape in the process. He was one of several innovators of the era who began to realise that the recording studio was not just a place where music could be recorded, but a means also of shaping what the music became. This was a way of thinking that held an enormous attraction for George. For both men, the studio was more than a technical stage of making records. It was a key part of the creative process. George, too, was to generate many miles of tape in his own recording career.

Zappa also made a point of going his own way in the business side of making music. He didn't care about hit singles and satisfying industry expectations. He was a maverick, an independent operator, devoted to musical rather than commercial success. George too had something of this in his make-up, frequently displaying casual disregard and disdain for the mechanics of the music business. He was not averse to commercial success, but he was not going to sell his soul to get it.

The music of The Mothers Of Invention, and Zappa's solo work of the period, was a deliberately concocted melting pot, often merging ideas and styles that seemed disparate. It was trashy, scatological and humorous; it was serious, challenging and thoughtful. It was rock'n'roll with jazz and modern classical elements thrown in. There was nothing straightforward about it. It was music that took unexpected turns and delighted in trampling over boundaries. These descriptions will all sound familiar to anyone aware of George's output in the 1970s – whether with Little Feat, as a session player, or as a solo artist. Cerebral, eclectic and sweaty are adjectives that would describe much of the music of both men. In the case of Zappa, the intellectual content seemed at times to be overpowering the heart of the music, but with George this rarely happened. He had something else as well. He had soul.

FIRST PRODUCTION JOB: THE GTOs

One last thing that George got from his spell with Zappa was a chance to produce an album. Normal musical terms should only be applied loosely to The GTOs (Girls Together Outrageously), an all-female "band" of notorious Los Angeles groupies. Their sole album *Permanent Damage* appeared under Zappa's patronage, with George taking on his first production job. The album got a mixed, even bemused reception and did not sell well. Best-known member Pamela (Miller, later Des Barres) went on to write the memoir *I'm With The Band – Confessions Of A Groupie*.

Various members of the Mothers appeared on *Permanent Damage* including keyboards man Don Preston and bassist Roy Estrada. The then-current line-up of The Jeff Beck Group, including Rod Stewart, also makes a showing, as does guitarist Ry Cooder and keyboardist Bill Payne. George described the experience as a lot of fun. "Interesting girls," he declared. "Their talent wasn't necessarily musical, but their lyrics were very interesting. I wrote or co-wrote two tunes."[26]

A couple of stories have circulated to explain why George left Zappa's employ. Both of them agree that Zappa asked George to leave, and that George was quite happy to go. Pamela Des Barres said he was kicked out for smoking dope, as Zappa himself was rigorously abstemious.[27] But the other, more frequently repeated story – indeed the story told by George himself – relates his departure to a song, 'Willin'', that he wrote some time in 1969.

'Willin'' would be George's first commercially successful song, and probably the one with which people still most readily associate him today. Zappa apparently liked the song but thought there was no place for it in the Mothers' set. By now he was no doubt aware of George's talent and ability. So, in the words of George, "It was decided that I should leave and form a band."[28] And that is what he did – although there were many months between leaving the Mothers and George finally putting together the first line-up of that band.

Meanwhile, as all of this was happening, a prodigiously talented 19-year-old keyboard player was hassling Zappa's camp, hoping to find a niche in his favourite band, The Mothers Of Invention. Bill Payne failed in that particular ambition, but as a result of hanging around Zappa's offices came into contact with George. The story goes that Payne went to George's house to meet the person who, he had been told, was putting a new band together. George was out, but Payne was let in by George's girlfriend. Impressed by the music and books on display, Payne felt an affinity for his future colleague before even meeting him. Precisely when this happened no one can now remember. (They couldn't even remember a few years after the event.) But given that it was after George had left the Mothers, it had to be during the summer of 1969. Now that Payne and George's paths had intersected, all the relationships necessary for the forming of what would become Little

Feat were in place. Lowell George and Richie Hayward already knew each other from The Factory, and George had met future Feat bass player Roy Estrada while in Zappa's employ, the two playing alongside each other in the Mothers. Estrada had worked for Zappa for several years. He was the bass player with The Soul Giants, the band that Zappa joined, took over and re-named The Mothers Of Invention in 1965. Estrada continued with the Mothers for the rest of the decade before becoming the last of the original four to join Little Feat.

So many of the threads that joined together with the forming of Little Feat could be traced back to George's spell in The Mothers Of Invention. Not only did three out of four members of the new band – George, Payne and Estrada – meet because George was in Zappa's band, but even the new band's name had its origins in that period. In an oft-quoted story, the name is credited to Jimmy Carl Black. He explains, "When Lowell George was in the Mothers, he used to room with Roy Estrada and myself. His feet were short and wide, so I told him that if he ever started a band he should call it Little Feet. They did name it that, but with the spelling Little Feat."[29] Richie Hayward said later that the band had spelled Feat with an "a" in homage to the spelling of The Beatles.

When George left the Mothers to start out on his own it marked the end of his musical apprenticeship. It had been an instructive few years. While with Zappa, The Standells and The Factory he had toured, written songs, made records, and even appeared on TV. He had experienced the less scrupulous side of the music business. He had demonstrated an emerging, enquiring creativity and a desire to control the creative process – something he had seen worked out successfully by Zappa. He had also met his three future band members. He was by then in his mid 20s, not a young age by the standards of the time to be putting a band together and looking for a deal.

CHAPTER 3

I'm Willin', oh I'm Willin'

"Lots of guys imitate Howlin' Wolf, but Lowell was one who really had something of Wolf in there."

JOHN SEBASTIAN

As the 1970s began there was a cultural vacuum between the broken dreams of the 1960s and the possibilities of a new decade. The gruesome horrors of Altamont and the Manson murders trampled over the vestiges of hippy idealism as the 1960s closed. The Beatles split; Jimi Hendrix, Jim Morrison and Janis Joplin died. The counter-culture lost too many figureheads too quickly to sustain momentum, and the experimentation and indulgences of psychedelia, which just a few years earlier had appeared so promising and novel, suddenly seemed passé.

Meanwhile, many surviving big-name artists were looking further back to traditional forms for their musical inspiration. The Byrds had journeyed from a Mersey-influenced folk-rock to psychedelia and space-rock in a few years. And then in 1968 they effectively invented country-rock – or at least sold the idea to a mainstream audience for the first time – with the *Sweetheart Of The Rodeo* album. Gram

Little Feat's first line-up (L-R): Richie Hayward, Bill Payne, Roy Estrada, Lowell George

Parsons, briefly a Byrd, had been a pivotal influence on that record. He went on to form The Flying Burrito Brothers with long-serving Byrds bassist Chris Hillman, and the new group released another country-rock masterpiece, *The Gilded Palace Of Sin*, in 1969. Many records are glibly described as seminal, but these two really do deserve the description.

At more or less the same time, country influences began to appear prominently in the work of Bob Dylan and The Rolling Stones. Following his sojourn in Woodstock with The Band that spawned *The Basement Tapes*, Dylan's 1968 album *John Wesley Harding* was stark, minimal and acoustic. In 1969 came his overtly country-influenced *Nashville Skyline*, which even featured a duet with Johnny Cash.

Psychedelia hadn't suited The Rolling Stones. The album they'd recorded in the style, *Their Satanic Majesties Request*, was a patchy anomaly, and when they released 1968's *Beggars Banquet* it was welcomed as a return to form. It was the last Stones album on which doomed founder member Brian Jones played. Dominated by louche, ragged, sleazy acoustic blues and country songs, dripping attitude and danger, it sounded distant from the pop hits the band had been turning out just two years earlier. The following year's *Let It Bleed* was more of the same, an equally strong album.

Parallel to all of this, The Band emerged fully formed, synthesising much of America's musical history in two albums. They had spent a decade on the road, trudging through the bars, dives and ballrooms of North America, all the time absorbing the nuances, traditions and sounds of many forms of American music. It was a long apprenticeship, but one that served them well. Their 1968 debut, *Music From Big Pink*, was a strikingly mature work; the eponymous follow-up a year later was even better. The Band were all multi-instrumentalists and singers, and the possibilities this offered enabled them to conjure a complex, interwoven acoustic-and-electric sound with rousing harmony vocals, delivering their often opaque, mysterious narrative songs. People would be saying much the same things about Little Feat a few years later.

As so often happens in the process of musical development, different people in different places were arriving at similar points at the same time. The Byrds, Dylan, the Stones and The Band were all artists who had grown up, musically speaking, through the 1960s, and all had ended the decade concocting their own unique blends of blues, country, folk, pop and rock'n'roll. As Bill Payne confirms, he and Lowell George were well aware of them – and much more music besides – as they prepared to launch their new band in late 1970.[1]

Although the George/Payne nucleus of Little Feat had come together in the summer of 1969, the band proper didn't really exist until a year later. The two had spent the interim writing songs, planning their campaign, playing the odd session, and waiting for drummer-elect Richie Hayward to leave The Fraternity Of Man. George had confidently persuaded the younger Payne that Hayward was their man, and that it was just a matter of waiting for the drummer to bow to the inevitable. They also auditioned somewhere between a dozen and 20 bassists. The second of these was one Paul Barrère, the younger brother of a classmate of George's from Hollywood High School. In fact, Barrère was a guitarist, not a bassist, so it's hardly surprising that he failed the audition.

As for the songs that George and Payne wrote in that formative year, some would appear on Little Feat's first album. Many others didn't, and are now forgotten. It was the songs that did make it to the first album that formed the basis of an "unplugged" set that George and Payne played in Lenny Waronker's Warner Bros office, a performance that got the band signed to the label some time during the summer of 1970. Bassist Roy Estrada had finally decamped from The Mothers Of Invention, and Richie Hayward from The Fraternity Of Man. The Feat were finally ready to start walking.

THE FIRST RECORD ALBUM

The band's eponymous debut album appeared right at the beginning of 1971, having been preceded a few weeks earlier by a single of two songs lifted from the album. It's a short album by today's standards, with 11 songs – 12 if you count the Howlin' Wolf medley of 'Forty Four Blues'/'How Many More Years' as two songs – and a total playing-time of just 33 minutes. Of those 11 songs, George wrote three and co-wrote five (four with Payne and one with Hayward). Payne contributed two of his own. Producing the album was Russ Titelman, who published the band's songs through his Abraham Music company. He also played piano on one song.

The album was engineered by Bob Kovach and Rudy Hill, with further mixing work done by Kovach. Ry Cooder and Sneaky Pete Kleinow also contributed, and Kirby Johnson arranged strings and horns. Sessions for the bulk of the album took place in the autumn of 1970, with a couple of the recordings dating back earlier than that. Apart from those exceptions, the album was recorded at United Western Recorders studio in Hollywood (where *Pet Sounds* had been made a few years earlier). Ry Cooder was making his debut album at the same complex and the same time.

Little Feat tends to be undervalued when compared to the rest of the band's recorded output. Within a few years of its release, George himself was in the habit of dismissing the album. His objections were focused on producer Titelman who, said George, wouldn't let the band into the studio for the mix, and abruptly curtailed the project for financial reasons.[2] The surviving band members indicated agreement with George's less than enthusiastic memories of the album when they represented it with only two songs on the career-spanning retrospective boxed set *Hotcakes And Outtakes* released in 2000; most of the later albums warranted four or five tracks apiece.

It is true that in parts the album sounds incomplete. Arrangements are often sparse, particularly compared to the multi-layered complexities of later Little Feat records, sounding as if short of an overdub or two. The production is rudimentary, and although theoretically a stereo record, some of the songs make such limited use of the facility as to be mono in all but name. Indeed, some of the cuts are no more than polished-up demos. But despite these obvious limitations, it was a far better record than many albums released that year. Furthermore, it includes a version of George's most enduring song, 'Willin".

LISTENING TO *LITTLE FEAT*

The album kicks off with George and Hayward meshing slide guitar and drums to introduce Payne's song 'Snakes On Everything'. It's a strong track, one of several mid-paced rockers, and contains most of the instrumental and production ingredients that feature on almost all of the rest of the album. The basic backing track consists of bass, drums, piano and double-tracked distorted slide guitar, the latter mixed very high. Payne's lead vocals are occasionally almost swamped in the mêlée, and work best when periodically sweetened with high-register backing vocals. Funky, stabbing horns complete the arrangement. Guitars dominate the left side of the stereo spectrum, with the rest of the instruments leaning to the right side. The lead vocals are then spread evenly across the two channels. Variations on this simple mixing technique are used throughout most of the album. The song fades just short of three minutes with drawn-out, ascending guitar notes.

'Strawberry Flats', a Payne/George collaboration, follows. This was one side of the single that had been released in late 1970 to herald the album. It's another mid-paced rocker, but this time dominated by rambunctious piano, with George's guitar providing supporting texture and detail apart from one short, loud solo. The stereo spread is the same as the preceding track. George sings the witty, lost-on-the-road lyrics with undeniably Jagger-like inflections in his phrasing: the delivery of the repeated phrase "not in my house, not in my house", complete with strangled harmonies, is pure mid-period Rolling Stones. The band's playing sounds live and just the right side of ragged, but is obviously well-rehearsed, as illustrated by the neat closing phrase which concludes the song at a little over two minutes.

Two songs in, and Little Feat are setting up their stall as a rootsy, bluesy rock'n'roll band with an affection for The Rolling Stones and a knack for carefully structured songs that sound conventional enough on first listen but don't always follow predictable verse/chorus structures. 'Truck Stop

Girl', the third song, introduces another dimension. It's a traditionally assembled country song, almost slow enough to be a ballad. Written by Payne and George, it has a straightforward verse/chorus structure varied only by a few different chord changes at the beginning of verse three. The narrative lyric tells the tragic tale of a truck driver's demise, with just enough left out of the story to create an air of unresolved mystery. Truck drivers, death, and an enigmatic woman in a bar are ingredients almost guaranteed to attract the attention of a country audience, and the song has indeed often been covered and remains popular. By the time Little Feat's version appeared The Byrds had already included it on their *untitled* album, making them the first big-name rock act to record a Lowell George song.

Payne says that on this song and his other collaborations with George their working relationship as songwriters was not delineated into strict roles and responsibilities. Each brought various ingredients to the process, maybe a few lines of lyrics, or some chord changes, and worked up the song together.[3]

'Truck Stop Girl' is another short song, just over two minutes. It starts without any preamble: the whole band and George's plaintive vocals come straight in at the first bar. Instrumentation is even more basic than the preceding two songs, consisting of just piano, drums and bass, with George contributing a barely audible acoustic guitar. A high, straining harmony is layered on top of George's lead vocal for the choruses. It says a lot about the abilities of Payne, Hayward and Estrada that they could create such a full, complete sound with such limited means. The use of the stereo spectrum is negligible, which reinforces the overall impression of unadorned, unpretentious simplicity. And although there is little in the way of innovation in either the way the song was constructed or its arrangement, it is so well executed that all that hardly matters.

From the conventional 'Truck Stop Girl' the album moves into one of its most unusual songs, the involved, elaborate ballad 'Brides Of Jesus'. Another Payne/George collaboration, the song's lyrics are almost completely devoid of easy-to-follow narrative qualities. Obvious meaning is deliberately avoided in favour of abstract poetic images, snatches of dialogue and biblical references that together conjure a spirit of yearning. Although conventional rock-ballad instrumentation is employed – the band's bass, drums, piano and acoustic guitar backing is bolstered by Payne's sepulchral organ playing and a swooping, lush string arrangement – the song's structure is complex and hard to predict. George's vocals are strong and assured. It's a strangely engaging song, and one that required a sizeable measure of musical competence and imagination to write. George and Payne never again composed anything remotely like 'Brides Of Jesus', which seems something of a shame given the song's melodic and dynamic qualities.

After the grandiose complexities of 'Brides' comes the record's simplest arrangement, the first Little Feat recording of what many still think of as George's best song, 'Willin''. The recording that appears on *Little Feat* was actually a dusted-down demo of the song that had first brought George to the attention of Titelman a year earlier. George would later say that the demo was recorded with the aid of Ry Cooder one morning at his home before he went on tour with the Mothers – which would date the recording some time up to May 1969. He also said that the original recording featured Gene Parsons of The Byrds on drums, and Russ Titelman playing piano,[4] although for the album it is stripped back to George's acoustic guitar and wayward vocal, plus Ry Cooder's slide guitar. The demo might not have been the first recording of the song, though, as Jimmy Carl Black from The Mothers Of Invention talks of another version, now lost, recorded "in my living room in Woodland Hills, California, with Roy [Estrada] on bass and me on drums".[5]

George recalled that 'Willin'' was written in Richie Hayward's house, although he was not specific about when. A chance remark about the "three wicked Ws – weed, whites and wine" followed by another remark about a chair that had been left outside and "warped in the rain" triggered a creative burst that left George with a lyric that fitted a tune he had written the previous day.[6] Black, though, tells another story: "He wrote 'Willin'' in room 16E of the One Fifth Avenue Hotel in New York in early 1969."[7] These two accounts don't necessarily contradict one another. Given George's predilection for re-working songs it's quite possible that Black heard George revising the original draft that had been written at Hayward's house.

Whatever the provenance of the song, George was later to rubbish the version on *Little Feat*, preferring the full band recording that would be included on the *Sailin' Shoes* album. (Some vinyl issues of these two albums have 'Willin'' spelled with the missing g: 'Willing'.) George drew attention to his out-of-tune vocals on the earlier take – the drawn out note on the word "wine" at the end of the chorus phrase "weeds, whites and wine" being a particularly noticeable example. In fact the song sounds like it is pitched several tones too low for George's natural range. But despite these shortcomings, the stark, skeletal ambience of the recording has a certain charm, and in the light of current alt country tastes even manages to sound contemporary more than 30 years after it was recorded. The appeal that makes it George's most-covered song is clearly evident even on this rudimentary version.

The mellow mood of the acoustic 'Willin'' is abruptly shattered by 'Hamburger Midnight' which follows. It's a greasy, dirty song full of car imagery, cranked into life by Hayward's sleazy, shuffling beat and driven by Payne's rinky-tink barroom piano. It had already appeared on the earlier single. George growls, howls and hollers in his best Captain-Beefheart-meets-Mick-Jagger vocal and slips in some sinewy, distorted slide guitar for good measure. The production harks back to the first two songs on the album, with piano dominating the left side, guitar and vocals the right, and drums across the spread. Both song and arrangement give the impression of barely controlled fury. Ed Ward, reviewing the single in *Rolling Stone*, described the song as "packed with incredible energy".[8] It's another short number, again only just over two minutes, and at 1:30 is interrupted by a brief multi-tracked talk-over of jumbled voices ending with George commenting about Big Macs.

'Hamburger Midnight' closes side one of the original vinyl issue of *Little Feat*. Listeners fresh to the album with no prior knowledge of Lowell George's earlier bands or Little Feat's single would by now probably be thinking about The Rolling Stones and The Band.

They would also be thinking that, in Lowell George, Little Feat had an accomplished slide-guitar player, such is the prominence of his playing so far. Of course, George did not just play slide guitar, either on this album, on other Little Feat records, or during the myriad sessions he performed throughout the 1970s. Yet it was as a slide player that George excelled, and it is his slide playing that is still recognised and revered today. George was one of few guitarists to evolve an instantly identifiable sound, with an exactness of phrasing, a ringing clarity, and a sustain that hints at the infinite. In the words of his friend John Sebastian: "I don't think Lowell understood how completely singular his guitar playing was."[9] But that singular style was still at a relatively early stage of evolution on *Little Feat*.

PLAYING THE SLIDE GUITAR

Slide playing differs from normal guitar playing in the way that the notes are sounded. Normally, guitar players hold down a string on to the guitar fingerboard in front of a fret (using the left hand for right-handed players). Playing slide guitar, however, involves touching the strings with a "slide" to pitch a note. In theory the slide itself can be almost any hard object of an appropriate size but is usually a metal or glass tube placed on a finger. George chose a typically idiosyncratic device to use as a slide – a sparkplug-puller. Slide guitarists often used bottlenecks for slides, which is why the term "bottleneck guitar" is used interchangeably with "slide guitar".

Once the note has been selected by placing the slide on the strings, it is sounded by the player plucking or hitting the string with their right hand in the regular fashion. Playing conventionally, if you fret a note correctly and the guitar is in tune you will always sound an in-tune note. But this is not the case with slide-guitar playing, where there is no obviously "correct" place to put the slide to achieve a particular note. For slide players, frets are only there as visual clues to where the notes fall on the strings. So it becomes crucial to be able to "hear" the note in order to be able to pitch it correctly. Consciousness of pitch is at the heart of good slide playing.The possibility of sliding to microtonal variables between the fixed semitones of fretted playing can make slide guitarists sound very distinctive. Players exploit this possibility to play glissandi, which means to swoop up and down between "correctly" pitched notes. For example, if a slide guitar player wants to sound a C note they might hit an A and then slide up to the C. In this sense, slide guitar is similar to country fiddle playing. The pedal-steel guitar popular in country music works on a similar principle, too, although pedal-steel guitars are laid horizontally on a stand or legs in front of the player and the "slide" is a metal bar held in the hand rather than a tube placed over a finger.

The deepest roots of slide guitar playing are lost in history, but the style is most commonly traced back to Hawaiian music, African-American culture, and early blues. Consequently, when slide guitar playing first started to feature regularly on rock records during the 1960s, it was understandable and appropriate that guitarists such as the late Duane Allman of The Allman Brothers paid homage to blues slide players like Elmore James. Although it was late in the decade before slide guitar became a regular sound on big-selling American rock records – The Allman Brothers started recording in 1969 – British blues-influenced bands such as The Rolling Stones and Fleetwood Mac had already been using the style for some years. By the time the first Little Feat album was recorded in 1970, slide-guitar playing was familiar to rock audiences.

LOWELL'S INJURED HAND

No one claims that George was the first white West Coast rock slide player. If anyone deserves that honour it is Ry Cooder. Duane Allman was apparently inspired to take up slide guitar after hearing Ry Cooder perform Blind Willie McTell's 'Statesboro Blues' with Taj Mahal.[10] Along with Spirit drummer Ed Cassidy, Cooder and Taj Mahal had been performing bluesy folk-rock as The Rising Sons since 1965. Cooder had also contributed slide parts to Captain Beefheart's 1967 album *Safe As Milk*. So although George was one of several West Coast musicians in the late 1960s exploring the possibilities of slide guitar, he was definitely not the first. But he was one of the first. As Barrère confirms, "He was the first one I saw playing slide in the clubs around Hollywood."[11]

It's often reported that George started playing slide as a result of injuries sustained in an accident with a model aeroplane during the recording of the first Little Feat album: George's hand was cut up by the model's propeller, which was powered by a small engine. Although this incident certainly happened, and the resulting injuries did prompt George to turn more frequently to slide guitar, he had already been experimenting with the style for some time before.

During an interview in 1976 George said that he'd been introduced to the idea of playing slide by an unnamed friend at an unspecified session "about six years ago",[12] indicating that he started playing in 1970. But it's too vague a reference to be reliable in pinpointing the exact circumstances in which George first took up playing slide, and when. Indeed the date he alluded to seems almost certainly incorrect. Jimmy Carl Black remembers George playing slide during his time with The Mothers Of Invention (1968 to 1969). Larry Tamblyn of The Standells recalls him playing slide on one of their songs (in 1968). Paul Barrère remembers that George played slide in The Factory (1965 to 1967), which is confirmed by fellow Factory-member Kibbee, who says that George started experimenting with the style in the last days of that band. However, nobody seems to remember exactly when George first put his socket wrench on the strings of his guitar, or what or who prompted him to do it.

Early recorded evidence of George's embryonic slide playing can be heard on a very obscure album by Ivan Ulz called *Ivan The Ice Cream Man*. It just pre-dates the first Little Feat album. Ulz was a jobbing songwriter and had been contracted to make a record for poet Rod McKuen's label, Stanyan. He recorded it in 1970 with the help of George, Payne and Jackson Browne, among others. George appeared on two songs. '1440 Broadway' is a bluesy romp about being lost and broke in New York, and features some competent if derivative blues slide playing, while 'Grand Illusion' is a three-chord dirge with more slide guitar, this time less accomplished and punctuated with the odd fluffed note.

George's slide-guitar style was at first like that of most other contemporary white slide players, tending toward a rock adaptation of the playing of Chicago urban bluesmen, along with some country inflections borrowed from pedal-steel guitarists. The electric and acoustic slide-guitar playing that was an integral part of The Rolling Stones' albums *Beggars Banquet* (1968) and *Let It Bleed* (1969) drew heavily on these influences. In fact, George's early slide playing bears a marked resemblance to the playing on those Stones records – although this would have been as much to do with sharing influences with the Stones' guitarists as copying their style directly.

Or perhaps, as some have suggested, the influence worked the other way as well. George is sometimes credited with playing slide guitar, along with Ry Cooder, on the soundtrack to the film *Performance*, which had Mick Jagger among its stars.[13] The movie and its soundtrack were produced in 1970. Some involvement from George seems plausible: the album was released on Warners, Little Feat's label, and Russ Titelman, then George's publisher, co-wrote one of the songs, 'Gone Dead Train', with Jack Nitzsche, who produced and arranged the soundtrack.

George's friend and songwriting partner, Martin Kibbee, believes that George took part. There is certainly plenty of slide guitar on the *Performance* album, although this is credited in the sleevenotes specifically to Cooder on most songs. Interestingly, though, no guitarist is credited for 'Gone Dead Train', despite the arrangement featuring a slide guitar player who sounds a lot like George at the time of the first Little Feat album. Randy Newman, who sang 'Gone Dead Train', says George did not play on the track.[14] Kibbee says that not only did George appear on that song, but on others on the album too.[15] Additionally, he suggests that the Stones directly copied Cooder and George when recording *Let it Bleed*. Whether this did happen or not, it would be quite incorrect to imply that the Stones stole their slide guitar style wholesale from Cooder and George, as the British band had already been using slide for many years. But maybe there was a mutual exchange of ideas. Certainly, a few years later the Stones publicly stated their admiration for George and Little Feat.

HOWLIN' WOLF AND THE REAL BLUES

Like many rock guitarists learning their trade in the 1960s, George was enthralled by the blues, in particular the electric blues of Howlin' Wolf and Muddy Waters and the acoustic blues of Robert Johnson. He said that the rhythm patterns found in Johnson's work were inherent to the music he wrote, although he did not consider Johnson as a direct guitar-playing influence. He also admired the playing of Muddy Waters, although again he did not consider this as a direct influence. And it's interesting to note that when George's colleagues are asked about the artists who had the greatest impact on him musically, the name that comes up most often is Howlin' Wolf – a musician not known primarily as a guitarist.

Physically imposing, commanding in performance, and sometimes threatening in manner, Howlin' Wolf (real name Chester Arthur Burnett) had rolled into Chicago in the early 1950s, already in early middle age, having performed part-time for many years while working as a farmer, among other things. A limited instrumentalist on harmonica and guitar, Wolf shone as a vocalist and performer, his vocal trademark being the mournful drawn-out howl from which he got his name. His harmonica playing was rudimentary and forceful – like the man's singing, its most recognisable characteristic was long-held notes stretched over several beats and even several bars. He used a number of guitarists during his long recording career, the most notable being Hubert Sumlin.

George was not unusual in admiring Chicago blues in general and Howlin' Wolf in particular. The Rolling Stones had insisted Wolf appear on the *Shindig* television programme with them when they first visited America. Among many British and American rock musicians it was a commonly worn badge of credibility to display a knowledge of the blues – and even to claim artistic kinship with such gritty embodiments of the "real" blues. The gritty embodiments themselves, however, tended to view this well intentioned but naive patronage with a mixture of contempt, resignation, opportunism and humour.

Unlike many white rock musicians, though, George was able, eventually, to imbibe these influences and create his own style from them. Crucially, he was able to develop a style of playing that respected the spirit of the originators without slavishly copying them. Most blues music is economical and direct, sometimes subtle and understated – and all these characteristics were present in George's mature style, yet largely missing from the ponderous bombast of much heavy rock guitar playing of the time, which nonetheless often professed to be "blues influenced".

George was too aware musically (and no doubt culturally) to claim that he was in any way "like" Howlin' Wolf and other bluesmen, but his admiration did go beyond the enthusiasm of many other young whites of the time. John Sebastian believes that George must have made considerable efforts to learn, understand and internalise the work of musicians such as Howlin' Wolf, to be able to imbue his own playing with something of that spirit while still maintaining his own identity. He went beyond copying and on to interpretation. "Lots of guys imitate Howlin' Wolf," says Sebastian, "but Lowell was a guy who really had something of Wolf in there."[16] Perhaps one influence that can be traced from Howlin' Wolf to Lowell George is the habit of "stretching" notes across bars. Wolf sang those notes and played them on his harmonica; George sang them and played them on his guitar. The already portly George may also have related to the 300-pound man sweating profusely on stage, consumed by his music.

George's devotion to Wolf was certainly genuine enough. Sebastian recounts a story about a young George going to see Howlin' Wolf play. "He goes to Santa Monica, I think it was, one of the little blues clubs, which has Howlin' Wolf for a night," recalls Sebastian. "Wolf puts on a typically amazing show, and afterwards Lowell goes backstage with his heart on his sleeve. He says, 'Mr Burnett, I'm so impressed, you've meant so much to me, and I've really tried to learn from you and reinterpret what I've learnt into my music, and I think maybe I've got a little bit of it in there.' Wolf gives him a long look … and says, 'Fuck you.'"[17] George was in the habit of telling variants of this story on stage with Little Feat during the 1970s. The insult was taken in good spirit, and George's enthusiasm and respect for the cantankerous veteran bluesman remained undimmed. Ira Ingber from The Factory days recalls George being particularly keen to collaborate with musicians if, like George, they were "versed in the ways of Chester Burnett".[18]

Six of the 11 songs on *Little Feat* feature slide playing. On two of these, parts are contributed by Cooder. George's three main slide guitar contributions – to 'Snakes On Everything', 'Hamburger Midnight' and 'Crack In Your Door' – are all deftly executed but give little indication of the individual style he was later to develop. The choice and use of technology – amps, effects and the like – has a big impact on a guitarist's style and sound, something George would later demonstrate to unique effect when he explored the sustain-giving possibilities of compression and delay. On *Little Feat*, though, he sounded like a lot of other guitarists of the time, using distortion as the primary means to achieve sustain, and spraying coarse blasts of sound into every gap in an arrangement.

FORTY-FOUR BLUES / HOW MANY MORE YEARS

On to the second side of the original vinyl issue of *Little Feat*, and a two-song medley that was George's most direct recorded statement of his admiration for Howlin' Wolf: Wolf's songs 'Forty-Four Blues' and 'How Many More Years'. Producer Russ Titelman called in Ry Cooder, who was working on his debut in the same studio complex, to play some slide guitar with George on the medley, the second of Cooder's contributions to Little Feat's debut after 'Willin''. Hindsight has polished up this incident, this meeting of two pre-eminent slide guitar stylists, until it gleams with the allure of legend. The truth, as captured in the grooves of *Little Feat*, is duller and more prosaic. Both players were yet to evolve their signature styles, although each was more than capable of rocking out with force, so musically the exchange is not as interesting as it would have been had it happened, say, three years later. Most listeners would probably conclude that Cooder's contribution could easily have been played by George, and vice versa.

The Howlin' Wolf medley is the least interesting track on the album, being both too derivative and too long to be of lasting interest and too often sounding like a bunch of people jamming on familiar songs that they love – great fun for them, less so for the listener. It is a notable recording, though, because it's the closest George got to paying direct tribute on record to one of his heroes. George's distorted vocal and harmonica, Payne's rock-steady piano riff, and Hayward's strong emphasis on the first beat of the bar on 'Forty-Four Blues' are all recognisable Wolf trademarks.

The next track, 'Crack in Your Door', returned the album to original material. Another George composition, it's a rather chaotic song that sounds like it might once have been a ballad that has since been speeded up. Indeed, a slightly slower earlier version would appear on the 2000 compilation, *Hotcakes And Outtakes*. On *Little Feat*, the now expected bass, drums, piano and guitar backing-track rumbles along behind another of George's Jagger-influenced vocals. A fuzzy blast of slide guitar punctuates the song before the last verse. Like 'Willin'' it was another song that developed in the months between an earlier recording (July 1969) and the album version (some time in mid 1970). The main differences were that some lyrics were edited from the revised take, and the section that starts "there's no need to follow …" is repositioned. On the first recording this is used as a chorus; on the second recording it appears just once, as the closing phrase of the song, immediately following George's slide-guitar solo, which is once again used as a dominant feature of the arrangement.

Next up is 'I've Been The One', a beautiful broken-hearted country-rock ballad by George containing the definitive country couplet: "I've tried everything that whiskey cures, but the pain endures." Sneaky Pete Kleinow from The Flying Burrito Brothers contributes appropriate pedal-steel guitar detail, while producer Titelman's piano credit presumably means that Payne didn't play. It's followed by Payne's big ballad, 'Takin' My Time', on which there is little evidence of any contribution at all from George.

The album closes with 'Crazy Captain Gunboat Willie', another Payne/George collaboration. Lyrically it's an oddball moral fable about a captain who abandons his crew, with dire consequences. Musically it's similarly eccentric and hard to categorise, at a tangent from the rest of Little Feat's output. The horn counter-melody has the off-kilter cheerfulness found on many mid-period Beatles recordings. George later said it was one of many Little Feat songs created by editing down a much longer, semi-improvised piece. It leaves the listener with a reminder that, for all the evidence to the contrary, Little Feat were more than a normal rootsy rock'n'roll band. There was no mistaking a quirky intelligence at work.

Outtakes not used on the original album include 'Rat Faced Dog' (Payne/George), another Stones-influenced blues-rocker, and 'Doglines' (Payne), neither of which are particularly interesting. Of more note is a fierce and ragged early take of 'Wait Till The Shit Hits The Fan' (Payne/George) which would appear in much revised form on *Feats Don't Fail Me Now*. It's an incomplete version, but against the more developed later "official" take illustrates again George and Payne's penchant for re-working and re-visiting ideas. (These all appeared on the 2000 compilation, *Hotcakes And Outtakes*.) Ed Ward's ecstatic review of the album's single in *Rolling Stone* had effectively announced Little Feat to the world in late November 1970, opening with the bold statement: "This is a masterpiece." He went on presciently to describe the music as sounding "like The Band taken once step further".[19] Bud Scoppa, writing in a New York magazine, also used the word "masterpiece" when reviewing the ensuing album, commenting that "there's something inexplicably strange and off-center about it".[20]

Little Feat may have been received enthusiastically by American critics, but it went unnoticed by most of the American record-buying public, selling a mere 11,000 copies on release – a dire showing for a major-label band at the time. A tour with Ry Cooder and Captain Beefheart did little to raise the group's profile. British music fans – presently absorbed with Led Zeppelin, The Who,

T.Rex and Rod Stewart – enjoyed some early exposure to Little Feat when DJ John Peel, always quick to champion a worthy lost cause, played the album's single on his BBC Radio-1 programme, though the album wasn't released at the time and so went unnoticed by all but the most vigilant of UK music writers.

By mid 1971 it was apparent to George, Payne and the rest of Little Feat that rock stardom was hardly imminent. Not for the last time, the band's future was hanging in the balance, their status as Warners recording artists in jeopardy.

So how does the *Little Feat* album stand up in the light of later achievements of the band and George? First, it cannot be dismissed as juvenilia. There is more to it than that. The songs are too mature and the playing too confident. And yet it is not the work of a fully formed band, and it is not a complete work in itself. Things might have been different if more studio time had been available to let George and the others develop the arrangements, or if George and Payne had been allowed more influence over the production and mixing of the record. There is still a sense of a band discovering their identity, and one yet to fully internalise their influences to the extent that these might be drawn on without being too obviously apparent.

Second, *Little Feat* is important as evidence of the collective nature of Little Feat at the time, both in terms of the band's ensemble playing and its shared songwriting credits. As Payne often points out, Little Feat formed as a band, not Lowell George and a collection of backing musicians. On *Little Feat* you can hear what he means. Indeed, Payne's own songwriting contribution was substantial, and his piano is at least as dominant an instrument as George's guitar on this early evidence. But that particular balance of power would not be maintained for long. Payne and George were never to collaborate as extensively again as songwriters, and this now seems like something of a missed opportunity given the strength of songs like 'Truck Stop Girl' and 'Brides Of Jesus'. For the next few albums, George would be in the ascendancy.

Over the years, the tension between collaboration and conflict would animate and ultimately pull apart Little Feat. Given George's already latent tendency to control, and given that Payne – and later Barrère – were too talented as musicians to settle for sidemen roles, collaboration all too often broke down into factionalism. But it was often when Little Feat worked as a unit, as a true band, that they were at their best. And there are many glimpses of that on the *Little Feat* album.

CHAPTER 4

Put on your Sailin' Shoes

"There was a flash of light, and I had it. It was a Zen experience."

LOWELL GEORGE ON WRITING 'SAILIN' SHOES'

Little Feat's career was in a perilous state after their debut album took a commercial nosedive. George had lost an ally in Russ Titelman, the two severing connections following disputes about their publishing agreements as well as Titelman's production of that first album. Furthermore, according to Van Dyke Parks, "Warners made no commitment after the first record and refused to finance a second one. Little Feat were in effect 'dropped' from the label."[1]

George was personally popular at Warner Bros thanks to his charm, but his band's tenure there seemed about to end before their career had ever really started. Parks had an office at Warners at the time and enjoyed a hard-to-define role in the company, working as a recording artist, session player and producer, among other things. He seemed somehow to manage to have influence without ever seeming like a true insider or company man. He kept, and still keeps, his credentials as a maverick

Lowell keeps an eye on that slide

intact. Parks's special influence was soon put to work in George's favour. Two explanations have been given for management at Warners relenting and allowing Little Feat the chance to record a second album. According to George's former colleague from The Factory, Martin Kibbee, it was 'Easy To Slip', the song they co-wrote that would open the forthcoming *Sailin' Shoes* album, that convinced the label that the pair had potential as writers and thus persuaded them of Little Feat's commercial promise.[2] Parks offers another story, saying he invited George to contribute to his album *Discover America* as a deliberate gesture of support. He says it was "the opportunity to play a pivotal role in Lowell's interpreted worth at the company".[3] George played guitar on that album, and Parks also chose to include a cover of the George composition that would become the title track of *Sailin' Shoes*.

Parks and George had first met when they were both playing sessions on the second album by Fraternity Of Man, the band that included Richie Hayward, Martin Kibbee and Warren Klein, all from The Factory. They started seeing more of each other after Little Feat's first album had been released, and their friendship and occasional musical collaborations became important to both men. Not only did George contribute to *Discover America*, but Parks would from time to time play an active role in George's career. His name appears periodically as a co-writer and producer on George's later records. He also acted as a sort of informal adviser on the business side of music, and indeed George credited him in that respect with "opening my eyes to a lot of things".[4]

Not only was Parks's role at Warners hard to define, his whole career, then and since, is unclassifiable. A bespectacled former child actor, he cut an eccentric, studious figure on the West Coast music scene of the late 1960s and early 1970s, darting between famous songwriting collaborations with Brian Wilson, playing innumerable keyboard sessions, and working on his own unique recordings. He knew all about poor-selling debut albums, too. His own *Song Cycle* was acclaimed as one of 1967's choice albums in *Esquire*, *The New Yorker* and *Time*, among others, and yet even toward the end of the following decade it had failed to sell more than 15,000 copies.[5]

Maybe that experience heightened Parks's sympathy for George's plight. Whether it did or not, it is clear that the two regarded each other as kindred spirits, and it is not hard to see why. Both were cultured, intelligent, articulate, observant, multi-faceted men with a tendency to a tangential approach to music. And both were obsessed with recording studio technique. To this day Parks speaks with great warmth about George, and of how he was compelled to try to help out at this stage in Little Feat's career.

The most tangible evidence of that assistance centres on the title song of the band's second album, *Sailin' Shoes*. Not only did Parks record it for *Discover America* to help bring George back into view at Warners, he also had a hand in its genesis. As is often the case, two slightly different versions of the nature of the collaboration are available, neither necessarily cancelling the other out, but more likely giving different perspectives and interpretations of the same events.

George's account goes like this: "I had some verses and I had some pieces of a chorus, but nothing was happening with it. Van Dyke came in and said, 'OK, let's play it,' and we sat down. He was at the piano and I had a guitar. We tried it once and then he said something to me – I can't remember what – and there was a flash of light and I had it. It was a Zen experience."[6] Parks says that 'Sailin' Shoes' was worked out during a session for *Discover America*. "Lowell came up with the title, and we extemporised the tune. I gave him the tape, and he took it back to [where he lived in] Topanga and returned in a week with a finished sequence."[7] The song ended up credited to George only, and Parks kindly chose to hold the release of his album until Little Feat's recording of the song came out on their new album.

RECORDING *SAILIN' SHOES*

The *Sailin' Shoes* album was largely recorded at Warners' Amigo recording studio, North Hollywood. Sessions began in April 1971 and continued intermittently until the end of the year, possibly even running a few days into 1972. Ted Templeman, a Warners house producer and former member of the 1960s harmony pop band Harpers Bizarre, was assigned to work with Little Feat. From the start he took an assertive lead role in the direction of the recording process and this inevitably led to some disputes with the controlling George. Despite that, though, the sessions were productive, and Templeman delivered an album with considerably more warmth, sonic depth, presence and variety than its predecessor. A single of 'Easy To Slip' backed with 'Cat Fever' was released in early January 1972 as a trailer for the LP, which followed a month later.

As with the first album, *Sailin' Shoes* has 11 songs, of which George wrote seven and co-wrote one (with Martin Kibbee) making this the Little Feat album most dominated by George's writing. Kibbee was credited under the pseudonym Fred Martin. He later said that this was because the two hoped to make a sly Beatles reference as the resulting credits would read George Martin. In fact Warners credited the pair's compositions to "George and Martin" or "Lowell George and Fred Martin" but never "George Martin", so the joke was lost on most people. Nonetheless, Kibbee would remain Fred Martin from this point on whenever he wrote with George (though we shall continue to use his real name).

Sailin' Shoes also saw the first appearance of the publisher's credit Naked Snake Music. This is a company started by George and Kibbee in an effort to keep track of publishing royalties, and still in existence today. George had had his fingers burned by unsatisfactory business experiences with The Factory, The Standells, The Mothers Of Invention and in the early days of Little Feat.

The album's one George/Kibbee composition, 'Easy To Slip', opens the record. Suitably for an album's trailer single, it is an overtly commercial song – superficially, at least. Kibbee had generated the initial idea during a sojourn in Europe which saw the break-up of his marriage. The song was completed by him and George on his return to America. 'Easy To Slip' has an introduction of acoustic guitar and drums, fleetingly reminiscent of the Stones' 'Street Fighting Man'. It develops with overdubbed electric rhythm guitar and Payne's chordal organ to create a warm, fulsome basis for both George's lead vocals and his typically concise slide-guitar solo. A fast but easy-going groove, lush harmonies, and Hayward and Estrada's dynamic playing give the song further momentum, and 'Easy To Slip' sounds like a hit. On the first impression, that is.

Closer examination reveals that the song does not have a chorus in the conventional sense. The "it's so easy to slip/it's so easy to fall" hook occurs just twice in the song, once at the beginning and once two-thirds of the way through. It's a catchy phrase, and would have borne regular repetition as a conventional chorus – which no doubt would have increased the commercial chances of the song when it was released as a single. That's probably what The Eagles or The Doobie Brothers would have done.

LOWELL'S WRITING STYLE

George often seemed reluctant to take the obvious route for a song's development, preferring instead unexpected twists, left-turns and tangential quirks. This tendency produces an unusual reaction in attentive listeners to many of his songs. On first hearing, the melodies are pleasing enough to imply a relatively traditional form of country or funk-influenced rock'n'roll song. There is little if any overtly avant-garde experimenting in most of George's writing.

But a closer, more analytical listening reveals that things are not what they seem. Chord changes might vary from verse to verse. The juxtaposition of verses, choruses, middle-eights and bridge passages isn't always predictable; sections of songs – whether they be verses, choruses, or something else – are repeated in a slightly different form, with perhaps the second verse having two more bars than the first, or some such variation. Things happen when you don't expect them to, but still sound like they are happening in the right place. Maybe it was this subtle subversion of the rules of pop and rock songwriting itself that would prevent George from having hits. Tellingly, his two most covered songs, 'Willin'' and 'Truck Stop Girl', are largely free from such compositional quirks.

An early, harder, rougher demo of 'Easy To Slip' – then titled 'Easy To Fall' – had been recorded in February 1971, now available on the *Hotcakes* compilation. This tape was pitched at The Doobie Brothers, but they did not take up the opportunity to record the song. It's another example of George's habit of revisiting songs, endlessly worrying at them, re-inventing and looking for new possibilities. The early demo version suffers from a rambling, raucous, overtly Stones-influenced arrangement similar to some of the more derivative playing on the first Little Feat album. The song itself has yet to develop the melodic appeal of the "official" take and particularly misses the section that precedes and follows the guitar solo on the later version, when Hayward creates the illusion of a change of pace by dropping out every other snare-drum off-beat.

But back to *Sailin' Shoes*. The next song is 'Cold Cold Cold' and it illustrates another of George's preferred ways of working, using tape editing as a part of the songwriting process. According to George the initial track was a 15-minute demo cut in drummer Hayward's living room. This tape was then taken into the studio, transferred onto the multi-track, edited, overdubbed – and became the song that appears on the album.[8] It was a process that George was to use frequently during his career. He would talk about the idea of using tape like a notepad, or a variation on that theme, in many of his interviews through the 1970s.

George's primitive drum machine, a Korg Donca Matic, is briefly audible at the beginning of 'Cold Cold Cold'. He used this device to keep time on his home demo recordings, and it can be heard on some of the previously-unreleased rough recordings that appear on the *Hotcakes And Outtakes* compilation. On 'Cold Cold Cold' it is audible for a mere 12 seconds before being obliterated by Hayward's pulverising tom-tom fill.

After this unconventional introduction the song settles into a medium-paced blues-rock work out, with George playing double-tracked slide guitar (one heavily distorted, the other cleaner) and Payne contributing both piano and electric piano. The song is melodically limited and dynamically somewhat mechanistic – no doubt as a result of playing to the drum machine that runs throughout the song (it becomes faintly audible again during the fade-out). But despite these limitations, 'Cold Cold Cold' works well as tough, straightahead bar-room rock'n'roll, reeking of sweaty attitude.

'Trouble', which follows, is both a change of pace and of texture, and is a more satisfying song melodically. It highlights yet another feature of George's writing, this time the introduction of unexpected images and abstract elements into apparently conventional lyrical themes and structures. It's a country ballad with an arrangement based on Payne's deft accordion and piano interplay. At first the lyrics seem in the classic country tradition, about the miseries of life piling up. But a few lines in and the protagonist is becoming nervous, eating too much, and ends up "so fat your shoes don't fit on your feet". A later reference to "footprints on the ceiling" confirms the subtle disturbance of what could seem just a pretty little acoustic ballad. It is a pretty acoustic ballad ... but the eccentricities remind the listener once again that something else, something a little strange, is going on.

Incidentally, George's friend Ira Ingber believes that one of his songs provided a line for 'Trouble', lifted when George was producing recordings for a band that Ingber was playing with at the time. "Nothing came of the recordings," he says, "but I'm pretty sure that Lowell took a lyric of mine that later appeared in 'Trouble'. The line was about 'footprints cover the ceiling'. He really liked the line. Really liked it! I'm glad he took it."[9]

By contrast, Payne and Hayward's 'Tripe Face Boogie', next in order, is a straightahead rock'n'roll song, one of two on the album along with George's 'Teenage Nervous Breakdown'. George again plays some clean-toned slide guitar on this cut, drifting inexorably toward his mature sound. This is most noticeable at the end of the solo, with George moving higher and higher up the neck, all the while sounding like he couldn't possibly find a higher note before managing just one more step up.

A similar guitar sound is used on 'Teenage Nervous Breakdown', a Little Feat live favourite that George recorded several times, although he later claimed to have developed a deep loathing for the song. An early version, later available on various compilations, pre-dates the first Warners sessions. It's taken at mid-pace and includes a much longer set of lyrics (which might explain why it is credited to George/Kibbee while later versions are just credited to George). On *Sailin' Shoes* the song is taken at a race, with George's frantic eloquence sounding like Eddie Cochran and Chuck Berry for a post-Dylan audience. "Some contend that rock'n'roll is bad for the body and bad for the soul," he sings. Payne's high-pitched right-hand piano improvisations reinforce the impression of 1950s rock'n'roll notched up by several degrees. Live, the band would find yet another gear, pushing the song until it seemed on the very brink of disintegrating in its own slipstream.

WILLIN', MARK TWO

The re-recorded 'Willin'' follows 'Tripe Face Boogie' and features a full band arrangement. George felt that the demo ambience of the song on the first album didn't do it justice. Listening to the two versions it's hard to disagree with him, in spite of the undoubted charm of that grainy, low-budget first effort. Much of the credit for the success of this second 'Willin'' must go to Payne. His effortless piano flourishes, especially when they intertwine with the first of Sneaky Pete Kleinow's pedal-steel appearances on the album, add an extra measure of poignancy to a song that, despite its defiant tone, has a built-in sadness. Hayward and Estrada provide solid backing, and George strums an acoustic guitar unassumingly.

Apart from singing the verses in a different order, George leaves the song itself unchanged. Wisely, though, he attempts only the first verse in the low range that he struggled with on the early version. In fact, George now almost talks the lyrics in that first verse – and on stage in later years he would literally talk it – because the notes required are so much lower than his comfortable range. This allows him to jump an octave into the first chorus, and when that is combined with a harmony vocal that joins at the same time on what is already a strong melody, the song has a real sense of opening up. Add in the alliterative placename poetry of the lyrics to this section – "Tucson to Tucumcari ... Tehachapi to Tonopah" – and there is enough happening to make the song distinctly memorable. There is hit-single potential here. Until, that is, George gets to the "weed, whites and wine" line – dope, pills and booze in one hit – ensuring that widespread airplay would be denied if the song were to be released as a single.

That particular act of commercial suicide apart, it's easy to see why 'Willin'' has proved to be such an enduring song. A simple structure, a mournful yet uplifting melody and a rousing chorus make for a good start. Then the lyrics combine traditional country subject-matter with more obvious rock'n'roll references, summoning the sort of romanticised blue-collar myth of truck-driver as modern day outlaw that captures imaginations on both sides of the Atlantic. The idea of driving "rigs" all night might not immediately make sense to a European audience – or even to middle-class Americans – but it has a romantic appeal nonetheless. The whole package amounts to a country rock classic.

Guest guitarist Ron Elliot, a former member of The Beau Brummels, joins in for the off-kilter, vaguely disorientating 'A Apolitical Blues'. George returns to his best blues vocal mannerisms to sing a lyric in which he refuses to take calls from Chairman Mao on account of the particular brand of despair referred to in the song's title. The juxtaposition of a classic blues structure with deadpan humour was another favoured George device of the period, an approach reminiscent of some of Dylan's work in the mid 1960s.

Next, the title track of *Sailin' Shoes* announces itself with an abstract line about a "lady in a turban and a cocaine tree" again worthy of *Blonde On Blonde*-era Dylan. The comparison occurs again when a deliberately out-of-time snare drum, played by George, gives the song something of the ramshackle feel of Dylan's 'Rainy Day Women Nos 12 & 35'. With its brooding verses and singalong chorus, 'Sailin' Shoes' would in much altered form become a live Little Feat favourite. The Van Dyke Parks version of the same song, recorded just before Little Feat's for his *Discover*

America album, locates much of the same tumbledown feel. *Discover* somehow manages, among many other things, to be a homage to Trinidadian music as well as the popular songs of the 1930s and 1940s with which Parks was so enamoured. Elements of these influences are present in his version of 'Sailin' Shoes', and they make an already strange song even stranger. Shorn of one of its verses, it's just over two minutes of unadulterated weirdness, with an arrangement featuring drums on the point of total collapse, marimbas, female backing vocals, and George's isolated slide-guitar chords.

On *Sailin' Shoes*, 'Teenage Nervous Breakdown' is followed by two Payne songs. 'Got No Shadow' has two characteristics that would come to feature heavily in Little Feat's sound later in the decade. First, the song itself hints at some of the jazzy textures that became increasingly apparent as more of Payne's songs were recorded on later albums. Second, there is a clear indication of the future direction of George's slide-guitar playing when at 1:44 he hits a note that sustains for a full ten seconds, hovering over the rest of the arrangement before plummeting back into the mix.

Sailin' Shoes marked a transition in George's emerging guitar style. His slide guitar, either electric or acoustic or both, appears on all but one of the 11 songs (the exception is the re-recording of 'Willin') and on many of these George completely forsakes the distortion that featured so strongly on the first album in favour of a clean, bright, pure tone. His playing was making use of the clarity and undistorted sustain that would later be such a big part of his unique style, though he had not yet achieved the full-bodied quality that was its other major ingredient. It would be on the next Little Feat album that the Lowell George guitar sound finally reached maturity – of which more later. Meanwhile, the second of Payne's songs on *Sailin' Shoes*, 'Cat Fever', credits George as arranger and features yet more of that evolving guitar sound.

The album's closing song 'Texas Rose Cafe' had again been pitched at The Doobie Brothers a few months earlier (the demo is on *Hotcakes And Outtakes*). The version they heard was a fractured, strangled blues with heavy guitar and an abrupt change of tempo. One can only assume that it must have caused some bemusement in the Doobies camp. On the *Sailin' Shoes* cut, recorded just a few months later, the song and the arrangement are much matured. But it is still an odd piece, devoid of anything resembling a traditional structure. A high-voiced, restrained first section leads into a more upbeat second which is itself in two parts. George adopts a more throaty singing style for this two-part section as he piles on the internal rhymes (fast car/jaguar/guitar, and so on). The second section then morphs into a mildly atonal psychedelic jazz freakout that lasts about a minute before abruptly lurching back into a reprise of the restrained mode of the first section. The song ends, anti-climactically, on a high note and a stray cymbal crash. It was an eccentric way to sign off an eccentric song, and a fitting way to end an unusual album.

Critical response to *Sailin' Shoes* in the US was again warm. Bud Scoppa in *Rolling Stone* praised Little Feat's versatility, songwriting and playing. "They never sound pretty," he wrote, "but there's an unmissable beauty about their rough-around-the-edges designs."[10] Unlike their debut, *Sailin' Shoes* was released in the UK, but made little impression. The public remained resolutely unmoved on both sides of the Atlantic, and the album sold only slightly better than its predecessor.

Why *Sailin' Shoes* wasn't successful isn't clear. The quality of the songwriting and playing far exceeded the work of most other Los Angeles bands of the period. An outtake from the album on *Hotcakes*, George's straightforward country-rock ballad 'Dorriville', is evidence of that. It's a song that would have been strong enough to warrant inclusion on most albums, but not *Sailin' Shoes*, such was the competition. Perhaps, as we've already suggested, music fans were confused by the group's tendency to assemble songs in an unconventional manner. Or maybe it was the fact that George, although by all accounts personally magnetic, lacked obvious, look-at-me rock star charisma when performing on stage or appearing in pictures. Whatever the reason, records weren't selling, times were hard, and no one was making any money out of Little Feat. Band members had to think of other ways to supplement a very meagre income, and George and Payne in particular started to accept frequent session work.

LOWELL THE SESSION-PLAYER

George had been playing sessions as early as 1969 and continued to do so until his death ten years later. He is known to have played on 40 or so albums (in addition to Little Feat's records) and became a noted gun-for-hire among the Los Angeles session elite. His most prolific spell was between 1972 and 1976 when more than half of his known session engagements took place. As well as the documented sessions there were undoubtedly many more appearances that went unreleased or uncredited. These alone constitute a fascinating minor sub-plot to George's story. There was a three-song recording with actress Ann-Margaret, who was intent on sounding like Tina Turner.[11] And a persistent rumour, strong enough to find its way into some rock reference books, has George playing flute and saxophone on Frank Sinatra sessions, although none of George's associates can corroborate this.

George himself mentioned that he'd worked on film soundtracks in the late 1960s, although it's frustrating that he didn't identify which movies.[12] In addition to George's possible contribution to *Performance* (1970) discussed in the previous chapter, Martin Kibbee recalls him playing on some of the film and TV scores of Kirby Johnson, string arranger on *Little Feat*, although he doesn't recall the titles.[13] And Michael Bruce of The Alice Cooper Group says that George wrote the untitled song that Alice Cooper performs in the film *Diary Of A Mad Housewife* (1970).[14] Cooper and George were both involved at the time with manager Herb Cohen.

The known, credited and recognised sessions together make up a substantial part of George's musical career, albeit one that generally passes unnoticed. Despite the fact that much of that work was taken for purely financial reasons, it is a mark of George's broad musical knowledge and sympathies that he was able to make always competent, sometimes telling, and occasionally exceptional contributions to albums by a very wide range of artists.

His sessionography makes for curious reading. It ranges from established names like James Taylor and Carly Simon to relative unknowns like Tret Fure and Cheryl Dilcher. He's heard in the polished disco/soul of Yvonne Elliman and the counter-culture weirdness of The GTOs, and appears on the vanity projects of rock aristocrats such as Bill Wyman and the releases of eccentric outsiders like Ivan Ulz. There's even Japanese experimental pop (Akiko Yano) to balance the more expected archetypal West Coast soft-rock (JD Souther). George's slide guitar graced them all. And he was still turning out for sessions after 1976, by which time Little Feat were shifting records and scoring chart albums. By this stage there must have been something in it for him other than money. No doubt there was a social element with much of this work, but his continued session playing is also evidence of George's sheer unabated enthusiasm for music. And, as Elizabeth George notes, it was nice to be wanted.[15]

In many ways the Los Angeles music business of the time was an incestuous, conservative, close-knit world. No doubt it still is. Familiar names crop up repeatedly as you glance through the credits of any number of records that came out of the city during those years. Producers would use players on recommendation and, if they did a good job, use them again on subsequent projects and recommend them in turn to friends. Thus contacts and relationships were made that led to interesting chains of connections, linking all manner of unlikely records over many years. George moved freely, easily and with confidence through all of this, liked and admired not only for his obvious musical skills but also for the enthusiasm and interest with which he approached the work of others.

Although many of these sessions meant no more than turning up at the studio for a few hours and laying down a crisp, brief guitar line, others involved commitments of days or even weeks at a time. And this happened alongside a touring schedule, regular songwriting, production work and Little Feat recording sessions that often turned into punishing endurance tests. It's not hard to see why the reserves of energy that he drew upon when juggling all these commitments started to fail him just a few years later, and why he often resorted to using artificial stimulants.

George was popular as a session player because he could be relied upon to turn up and put the right notes in the right places with little fuss. But although his work was always professional, many of the records he appeared on are not particularly distinguished. Additionally, George's role in many of these records was minor. But there are notable exceptions, examples of pristine guitar-playing or one-off songwriting partnerships that show George at his best. British writer Richard Williams picks out the Lowell George/John Sebastian song 'Face Of Appalachia' from the Sebastian album *Tarzana Kid* (1974) as one of George's finest moments on record. Another example is his guitar playing on John Cale's 1973 album *Paris 1919*, an important if understated contribution to an all-time classic record. (Both of these LPs as well as some of his other session work are discussed in more detail in later chapters.)

Artistic achievements aside, it should be noted that many of the albums George contributed to were big chart successes. Between the release of *Sailin' Shoes* in February 1972 and the sessions later that year for *Dixie Chicken*, George worked on Carly Simon's *No Secrets*, which would be a number-one US album and featured her worldwide hit single 'You're So Vain'. He played on one song, 'Waited So Long', contributing simple, swooping, drawn-out notes throughout. The sound is full, very sustained and drenched in reverb. He was very close now to his mature sound.

THE SLEEVE ART OF NEON PARK

Aside from the music, *Sailin' Shoes* was a noteworthy album for the first appearance of another key member of Little Feat's extended family, sleeve designer Neon Park. Born Martin Muller in 1940, Park had first come to George's attention for his garish cartoon cover of Zappa's *Weasels Ripped My Flesh* – and thus marked another pivotal relationship in George's career that can be traced back to his brief spell with Zappa. The two met later when Ivan Ulz, a friend and occasional collaborator of George's, picked up a hitchhiking Park and took the artist to George's house. Park would design the group's album sleeves from *Sailin' Shoes* onward, until his death in 1993, and his darkly humorous juxtapositions of seemingly incongruous elements served as a pertinent visual interpretation of Little Feat's music.

Park placed an anthropomorphic iced cake with, legs, arms and eyes on the cover of *Sailin' Shoes*, sitting it on a swing in an ornamental garden. This image related to the originally proposed title for the record, *Thanks I'll Eat It Here*, a fact explained in George's rambling and largely punctuation-free notes that appeared on the rear sleeve of the record. These too would become another regular feature on Little Feat albums. In fact, George would resurrect the unused title for his only solo album, seven years later.

George thought *Sailin' Shoes* was a big improvement on the promising but flawed debut. Most others agree, and the album has worn well. Many fans and critics still rate it as among the best of Little Feat's LPs. Some go further and think of it as the truest representation of George's musical vision. But the fact remains that one record alone can never do justice to the man's creative efforts. He tended constantly to evaluate, develop and innovate, making such a static summary view of his work flawed by definition.

But it is fair to say that *Sailin' Shoes* was a reasonably accurate representation of George's aspirations and ambitions at the time. And along with *Dixie Chicken* it is one of the two Little Feat records over which George had most influence. It's interesting, then, that one person who was not so happy with the album was Bill Payne.

A few years later, Payne said: "I played a lot on [*Sailin' Shoes*] but I was personally unhappy with it, because things didn't come out the way I heard them in my head."[16] No one would have thought it at the time, but with the benefit of hindsight this looks like one of the first cracks in what would become a huge creative chasm between George and Payne, a chasm that would eventually divide Little Feat in two.

Sailin' Shoes was both the pre-eminent work of the first line-up of Little Feat and a transitional record. George's singing style was moving away from the more overt imitative characteristics sometimes evident on the first album. His guitar playing, too, was becoming more recognisable. But there were still plenty of moments on the album when the music could clearly be categorised as part of this or that genre. It was not until after the album's release that events led to the band developing a sound that was always unquestionably Little Feat's alone.

During a dispiriting tour to promote *Sailin' Shoes,* bassist Roy Estrada left the band to join Captain Beefheart. Two reasons have been given: one, that Estrada wanted more of a musical challenge than he felt Little Feat offered; two, that Beefheart was offering a regular weekly wage. The second reason alone would have been a powerful incentive as Little Feat were at this stage still impoverished hopefuls. The parting seems to have been amicable enough. A few years later George was speaking fondly of his erstwhile colleague. "He's the sweetest guy ... If you know of any groups that need a bass player, he's one of the finest, he really is."[17] Estrada's departure could have been a decisive blow to the morale of a band still struggling with poor sales, little record-company support, and a low public profile. George turned it into an opportunity to further his musical vision.

CHAPTER 5

In the Bathtub...

"Lowell was a real musician. He knew a lot about music, both serious and non-serious."

VAN DYKE PARKS

When it came to music, Lowell George was a "deeply contemplative man"[1] says Van Dyke Parks. He liked to consider things from every angle. And the departure of Roy Estrada gave George the opportunity to reflect on Little Feat's progress up to this point: to reconsider, to experiment, and to revise the band in accordance with his ever-evolving musical ideas.

By now, having made two Little Feat albums and performed many sessions, George could think of himself as something of an old hand, both as a bandleader and a studio musician. He was growing in confidence, and that equipped him to take two bold steps that would have a dramatic impact on Little Feat's music. First, he wangled his way into the producer's chair for the band's third album. Second, as well as replacing departed bassist Estrada, he recruited two additional musicians. The first of these three new band members, Paul Barrère, had already played a bit-part in the Little Feat story. He had been briefly considered for membership in the band's formative days, before their debut release, when

The new six-piece Feat (L-R): Payne, Hayward, Clayton, Barrère, Gradney, and seated George.

he'd auditioned for the bass guitarist's vacancy that was eventually occupied by Estrada. Then, when Estrada left, Barrère had another go, although he seems to have approached the audition with little enthusiasm because he wasn't a bassist at all, but a guitarist. Once again he failed, and once again he was persuaded, by Little Feat's road manager Rick Harper, to make another approach. This time, though, Barrère offered his services as a guitarist. He prepared diligently, learning all the rhythm-guitar parts and some of the lead-guitar lines from *Little Feat* and *Sailin' Shoes*. That work paid off and Barrère was accepted into the ranks at the third attempt. The arrival of a second guitarist was to have a crucial impact on the development of the sound of Little Feat, as well as on the playing of George, who was now free to concentrate almost exclusively on lead slide parts.

So Little Feat had a new guitarist, but they were still without a bassist. That particular problem was solved by hiring Kenny Gradney, fresh from a stint with Delaney & Bonnie. Gradney's audition was a five-hour jam at the Warner Bros soundstage in Los Angeles. As a player, Gradney tends toward understatement and economy. He is the master of the perfectly placed phrase. So it was no surprise that he appealed to the similarly disciplined George. Once the new bassist had been accepted he in turn put forward for consideration his former Delaney & Bonnie colleague, conga player Sam Clayton. Clayton had been fired from Delaney & Bonnie because he was unable to play for a while after injuring a leg, an event that led to Gradney's resignation in protest at what he felt was the unfair treatment of his friend.

George hadn't been looking for a conga player but immediately recognised the polyrhythmic possibilities of having another percussionist to complement Hayward. Conveniently, also, Clayton and Gradney were from New Orleans, and George was interested in the New Orleans funk/soul of musicians like Allen Toussaint. Payne too had interests in this direction, having long nurtured a regard for New Orleans pianists such as Fats Domino.

It quickly became apparent that Gradney, Clayton and Hayward worked well together. Hayward had been in demand for sessions since 1972 (and still is 30 years later). He is able to maintain seemingly opposing drumming styles in creative tension, combining the physicality and aggression of rock playing with the jazzman's lightness of touch, the solid groove with complex fills. When Clayton adds his congas and other percussion instruments, a new layer of detail and extra emphases emerge, giving the songs even more momentum and energy than they might already have. Gradney, for his part, is the perfect foil for the other two. His lean and direct bass phrases serve as the solid foundation upon which Clayton and Hayward can build their elaborate percussive constructions. The three went on to become one of the most inventive and versatile rhythm sections in 1970s rock, contributing greatly to the unique ensemble sound that Little Feat generated during the band's often extended excursions on-stage as well as for the more precise requirements of the recording studio.

The importance of these changes to the personnel has diminished with time. It was this new line-up that went on to make a commercial breakthrough, and became the Little Feat that most people remember. And with hindsight, the three new members themselves look like predictable choices. Gradney and Clayton came as a pair, their arrival directly linked with Payne and George's interest in the New Orleans sound. Barrère, on the other hand, shared a background with George (they'd been to the same school). But at the time, the expansion of Little Feat from a subtly strange four-piece country-rock band to a six-piece multi-ethnic, multi-faceted rhythm machine was a radical transformation. It was a big surprise indeed to anyone who cared.

SEBASTIAN, GEORGE & EVERLY

However, if some of George's other fleeting notions for revamping the band at that time had come to anything, there would have been even bigger surprises. His quest for new musicians during the period of appraisal after Estrada's departure was to take some unexpected turns. Phil Everly, one half of The Everly Brothers, was briefly considered as a new member, along with the former leader of The Lovin' Spoonful, John Sebastian.

The Everly Brothers had been very big stars just a decade or so earlier, scoring a string of worldwide hits with their close-harmony, country-tinged rock'n'roll in the late 1950s and early 1960s. Changing fashions and a well-publicised sibling rivalry had diminished their standing as the 1960s progressed, and by 1972 they were in terminal decline, appearing as anachronisms from another age.

George came across Phil Everly, the younger brother, when Everly was working with Sebastian on an album project at Sebastian's house, at the same time as Sebastian and George were seeing a lot of each other. Sebastian played George a cassette of himself and Everly singing together, which set George thinking. "Phil had this beautiful high voice," said George, "John had a contralto, and I had a tenor that fit right in the middle. It was a nice vocal blend."[2]

Sebastian takes up the story. "I had attended one Little Feat rehearsal, with equipment. I wouldn't say I was being auditioned or anything, I was just there and I was playing. Certain parts of what I played entertained Lowell. He liked the idea that I had a rudimentary blues style that wasn't changed much by rock'n'roll. There came a point when he said, 'OK, I've lost a few members recently and I'm trying to restructure [Little Feat] – what if you and Phil joined?'"[3]

No doubt the strange concept of forming a harmony trio of a 1950s teen idol, a 1960s folk-rock star and a not-yet-happening 1970s rock star to front a newly funky country-rock band appealed to George. The unlikely threesome did get together once and sing. But not surprisingly the idea came to nothing. In fact, according to Sebastian, the whole episode was little more than a casual idea quickly dismissed – but it has become a story that has gained power and status among Little Feat fans through repeated retelling over the years. Nonetheless, it does underline George's willingness to try things out, regardless of how outlandish they might seem, just to see what would happen. He was, says Sebastian, "fearlessly experimental".[4]

THE SOUND OF THE SIX-PIECE

The antecedents of the new Little Feat sound are hard to pinpoint. What had been an identifiably West Coast country-rock group taking cues from The Band, Howlin' Wolf, Captain Beefheart and The Rolling Stones had now relocated itself, spiritually if not geographically, to another place altogether. That place was somewhere closer to the southern swamp boogie of Dr John and the infectious funk of The Meters. The impact of Gradney and Clayton's playing was to take what had sometimes been a rather hectic band and slow it down sufficiently to find a new funk swing. In the words of a song Clayton contributed to the *Down On The Farm* album some years later, Little Feat learned to "feel the groove".

Payne talks about "drawing a line between Stravinsky and Howlin' Wolf".[5] That is more than just a good interview quote – it says something about the tendency he and George shared of co-opting yet more influences and strands of music into a unique whole, of identifying connections and creative possibilities in apparently disparate elements. This tendency had already been evident in Little Feat's career so far, and in George's own musical development prior to Little Feat. The introduction of the New Orleans funk sound to Little Feat was another decisive step forward in the band's moves to blend genres – and a decisive one at that.

In the words of Parks, "Lowell was a real musician, from an academic standpoint. He knew a lot about music, 'serious' and 'non-serious'."[6] George's idea of applying this accumulated knowledge to his work with Little Feat was a deliberate and conscious process as much as it was intuitive. Sebastian's own 1960s band The Lovin' Spoonful had been formed with similar ideas about joining up many elements to create a whole, and it was something he and George discussed frequently at this time. "Lowell found a tremendous amount of comfort talking to me about this idea of a band that had a homogeneity that I think he saw in the Spoonful," says Sebastian, "in that the Spoonful too borrowed freely from country music, blues, and so on. I think Lowell also felt that freedom to stretch the boundaries of what a band could be."[7] Just what the band could be was becoming quickly apparent. The new Little Feat – it was a new band as much as it was a development of an existing band – fostered a style of exuberant ensemble playing that fed on itself, each member contributing ideas that would stimulate the others, and so on, round and round.

Rehearsals were concentrated and extended, and Little Feat became so tight they could afford to play loose. It was a period of burgeoning creativity. Songs often originated in those long rehearsal improvisations which were recorded, considered, edited, re-worked and moulded into the shapes that would become so familiar to followers of Little Feat. Indeed, many of the songs from this period would quickly become on-stage favourites – and indeed they remain so still for the present line-up.

The funky rhythm machine that Little Feat had become played their first gig for 40,000 people at the Diamond Head Crater Festival in Hawaii on April 1st 1972. It was an auspicious debut, but any thoughts that the new members might have had about instant wealth and fame would have been unfounded. It would be some time before they started to sell enough records to be considered more than a minor cult. Until then there would be much hard graft, on the road and in the studio.

IF YOU'LL BE MY DIXIE CHICKEN

The third Little Feat album, *Dixie Chicken*, was the first release by the six-piece line-up. It was recorded and mixed in late 1972, primarily at Clover Recorders, Hollywood. Engineers Robert Appere and Michael Boshears assisted George, the newly ensconced producer. It is a testament to his powers of persuasion and the strength of his vision that George, at this stage very much a novice producer, was able to persuade Warners to allow him to take control of a third album by a commercially failing band. The temptation to pull in a tried and trusted name to give the new album a commercial gloss must have been considerable, not only for Warners but George himself and the rest of Little Feat. But George's wishes prevailed, and he found himself in charge of proceedings.

As well as wielding a producer's power, George once again dominated the songwriting credits, although his contribution was smaller than on *Sailin' Shoes*. Of the ten songs on the album, George wrote five and co-wrote two (one apiece with Kibbee and Payne). Payne's contribution was limited to this co-credit with George and another co-credit with new boy Barrère. The remaining two songs were covers, one an Allen Toussaint song, 'On Your Way Down', while 'Fool Yourself' was written by future Little Feat member Fred Tackett.

George established a method of working for the recording of most of *Dixie Chicken* where songs were captured during brief live-in-the-studio sessions and then were extensively revised and honed through a lengthy overdubbing process. These were the two poles of George's working style, representing both his love of the spontaneity of live playing and the opportunities for control that were offered by working in the studio. The principle was simple: to capture a good basic live performance that could then serve as a foundation on which a more detailed and ornate edifice could be constructed.

It was a long and difficult process, and one not always relished by the rest of the band. Barrère described it as "making everything perfect"[8] and recalled occasions when Hayward's drum parts were created by tortuously recording one drum at a time. Why the process became such hard work was no doubt a combination of factors, George's perfectionism and his relative inexperience being two. Perhaps, also, his role as both band member and producer confused the decision-making process. Laying down the law in the way Templeman had done on *Sailin' Shoes* would always be easier for an authoritative outsider than an inexperienced insider.

Yet despite the painful process, George's production of *Dixie Chicken* was a success. He achieved a commendable clarity amid the fullness of sound created by the complex layers of instrumentation. But it was success achieved at a cost. George viewed the whole experience somewhat ruefully. A few years later he said, "The mania we had on *Dixie Chicken* ... that was hell on wheels, we were forever trying to finish that record."[9] Such was the physical effort involved in maintaining concentration for long sessions that George became ill after the final mix was completed. He said later that "the album took five years off my life".[10] With hindsight that statement has an ominous ring about it, as George's exhausting working habits – which involved many late nights alone in the studio, sustained by stimulants, following long days working with the band – surely contributed to his early death.

George's assumption of the producer's role enabled him to realise his ideas more faithfully, but it exacerbated underlying tensions within the band that would eventually erupt into a power struggle. His chosen method of building up recordings did not always meet with the approval of his bandmates, and his new role physically separated him from them as well. His usual practise was to sit in the control booth while the rest of the band recorded the backing track out in the studio's live room. George would then record his contributions later – something that was made easier by Barrère's arrival.

The new guitarist provided most of the rhythm guitar, while George was now free to concentrate on his lead slide playing. Rhythm guitar parts depend for success in particular on their interplay with the bass and drums, and so are best recorded live in an ensemble setting (although on *Dixie Chicken* George was prone to re-recording them himself later). The slide parts, though, were more easily woven into the fabric of a recording after the basic arrangement had been agreed – and this became a sometimes lengthy process that George liked to work through in his own time.

What all of this amounts to is that by the time of *Dixie Chicken*, George – as lead singer, lead guitarist, main songwriter and producer – was indisputably Little Feat's commander-in-chief. That is not to say that the other members were not able to contribute creatively, as indeed they did. But at this stage in the band's life the relationship between George and the others was not an equal one. George was able to lead things his way, and the band seemed willing to follow. That didn't last, although for a while it worked well enough.

SINGING *DIXIE CHICKEN*

The dense layers of instrumentation and harmonies that are a feature of *Dixie Chicken* are not just a result of the various contributions of the six band members. George brought in no fewer than four additional musicians and six female backing singers to assist with the project, including the previously mentioned Fred Tackett. Tackett had known George since the late 1960s when the two had met at a party at songwriter Jimmy Webb's house. Through the 1970s Tackett was a Los Angeles session regular, often appearing alongside George and Payne, and a songwriter. When Little Feat reformed in the 1980s, some years after George's death, Tackett joined the ranks as a guitarist alongside Barrère – a position he still occupies at the time of writing. On *Dixie Chicken* he contributed acoustic guitar.

The six backing vocalists included Gradney and Clayton's former employer, Bonnie Bramlett, and long-time Feat associate Bonnie Raitt. Raitt was a friend of George: he helped on some of her albums, and she would sing back-up on several Feat albums following *Dixie Chicken*. A less familiar name is Tret Fure (misspelt Trett on the album-sleeve credits). Fure was a relative newcomer to the music business, her previous experience limited to collaborating with The Spencer Davis Group on their 1972 *Mousetrap* album. She and George had met that year, and George went on to produce her eponymous solo debut in 1973, at the time only his second production credit (after 1969's GTOs album) outside Little Feat.

George's own singing style was developing away from the early recordings where his phrasing was sometimes derivative of Jagger, Beefheart and the blues. Even on some of the harder-edged material, a softly husky soulfulness was newly apparent in his voice. Barrère thinks that George was predominantly an intuitive singer and that the languid movement in his phrasing that became apparent on *Dixie Chicken* was very much a matter of feel, an indirect consequence of absorbing all manner of influences. That said, George also paid consciously careful attention to how other singers worked. One of the vocalists George was aware of and respected was Danny Hutton, lead singer of Three Dog Night, one of the most successful American bands of the period. Hutton himself was, as we shall see, to make a small but important contribution to *Dixie Chicken*. He describes George's voice as becoming "very fluid"[11] around this time. It's an appropriate description, and one that could also be applied to George's guitar style.

Although the precise beginning of George's slide-playing career cannot be determined (see chapter 3), *Dixie Chicken* is the Little Feat album on which his mature style first appeared. Almost all of the slide guitar on the album – and there is a lot of it – disposes of the more traditional approaches that George had employed on earlier records. Rather than semi-improvised blues-based solos, George carefully constructed what are essentially simple tunes and riffs. This was more radical than it seems. Unlike many guitarists of the period, George seemed intent not on grabbing every opportunity to play as many notes as possible, but rather was concerned with creating parts to complement the song. And if that meant a part consisting of only a few notes, and with lots of space between those notes, then so be it.

Most of these parts were either pure lead breaks, or counter-melodies to complement the vocal tune. Examples of the first category can be heard on the drifting instrumental 'Lafayette Railroad' and the rocking 'Two Trains'. 'Lafayette Railroad', a Payne/George collaboration which closes the album, is an exercise in tasteful restraint. The guitar plays the main tune, and George develops this using sustain so highly developed as to make his Stratocaster at times sound like a continuous tone producing instrument such as an organ. He allows the tune to evolve through successive repetitions – it is not simply repeated note-for-note each time it appears – but without ever allowing it to stray so far as to sound like it is wandering. The listener is always conscious of the original theme that is being expanded upon. And it is always a tune, not a more abstract "guitar solo". To make a comparison from another age and another country, it is a guitar part as definite, memorable and simple as something by Hank Marvin of The Shadows.

A buzzing slide chord that fades in like an approaching swarm of insects over Clayton's chattering congas announces the rollicking, funky 'Two Trains', a George composition. George then goes on to punctuate the song with two brief, simple lead breaks that demonstrate how far removed he was from many other rock guitarists then operating. The longest of these breaks is a mere 12 seconds, and both consist of a handful of notes shaped into complete, neat tunes, perfectly placed as the song dictates. No pyrotechnics, no over-bearing egotism, no overstaying his welcome. Typically, George resists the temptation to launch into an improvisation over the song's extended fade, preferring instead to settle into the groove with the rest of the band.

DIXIE CHICKEN TRACK BY TRACK

The title track of *Dixie Chicken* opens the album and was one of the songs that had evolved through many hours of rehearsal. George was an inveterate recorder, very much in the habit of making home demos and rehearsal tapes that he then shared with valued friends and collaborators, always interested to hear their opinions on these works in progress. Sebastian was one such friend, and he got to hear an embryonic version of 'Dixie Chicken'. "Lowell had a wonderful kind of a rumba rock feel," says Sebastian, "and between Kenny and Sam he could really express that. But for some reason the process of recording had drained the rumba part of that feel out of the original recording – and that was the feel that made it wonderful for me, so I began recording the song for myself with the idea of maintaining that."[12] The recording of 'Dixie Chicken' that Sebastian refers to appeared on his obscure 1974 album *Tarzana Kid*, which would also feature 'Face of Appalachia', one of George's best songwriting collaborations outside Little Feat (see chapter 6).

Little Feat's own recording of 'Dixie Chicken' introduces listeners to most of the characteristics of their new sound. There is Gradney and Hayward's brief syncopated introduction overlaid with Payne's barrelhouse piano riff and some loose slide-guitar licks. Then George's understated vocals appear in the verse, with massed female voices joining for the singalong chorus and a repeated slide guitar phrase punctuating the song after the second and third choruses. This is the essence of the new Little Feat compressed into just under four minutes. It was released as a single in March 1973, but true to the now well established Little Feat tradition, it saw no chart action.

'Dixie Chicken' is followed in the album's running order by 'Two Trains' (see opposite) which shares many of the same features. The third song, though, would have been more familiar in style for the experienced Little Feat listener coming to the new album. 'Roll Um Easy' is one of George's great ballads, a solo recording in all but name. He sings and plays both acoustic and slide guitar. Three Dog Night's Danny Hutton is the only other person involved.

Hutton and George were good friends and saw a great deal of each other socially. The two had been introduced by their mutual friend, Van Dyke Parks. "We just started hanging out together," says Hutton. "He used to come over all the time late at night on his motorcycle. It was not a musical relationship; it was more of a friendship. I had a music room downstairs that was all blacked out – black windows – and you could be in there all night and not know the sun was coming up. We used to sit there and play, and we tried to write together once in a while."[13]

Hutton's involvement in 'Roll Um Easy' began when he dropped into Clover Recorders studio one night to see George. Hutton had just completed a particularly arduous spell on the road with Three Dog Night. George was alone in the studio, working on 'Roll Um Easy', and was looking for a harmony vocal part. Hutton says, "I was sitting there and my voice was completely gone – I'd just come off tour. Lowell said, 'Come on in and sing,' and I said, 'Ah, man, I don't even think I can hit the notes.' He said to come on and try, and I sang it once and he said, 'Oh, I love it!' I asked to let me do it again, but he said no, he wanted it just like that. It was a complete accident."[14]

Accident or not, Hutton had contributed to a defining moment in George's career. One of his simplest compositions, 'Roll Um Easy' has the mysterious internal logic of all the great songs, sounding complete and just right. Despite its apparent simplicity it is irregularly constructed, running through a double verse of 16 bars, a 14-bar chorus, a single verse of eight bars, and a final 16-bar chorus. It tails off on the same lone, gently-picked acoustic guitar figure that started the song, shuffling quietly to a halt at 2:30. The arrangement is as sparse as that first recording of 'Willin'' on *Little Feat* – an acoustic guitar overlaid by spectral, weeping slide parts, though here played by George rather than Ry Cooder. The sparseness of the arrangement gives listeners a chance to savour George's new guitar sound, the two-note chords that drift over the closing phrases providing a particularly clear example.

George's understated vocal performance locates genuine emotion in a rock'n'roll-outlaw lyric, albeit a literate one, that could have sounded clichéd from a less sensitive singer. "I am just a vagabond / A drifter on the run / And eloquent profanity / It rolls right off my tongue." George was right to keep Hutton's hoarse harmony, which effectively counterpoints his own soft, breathy, close-miked intimacy. It's easy to understand why George considered 'Roll Um Easy' the most fully realised song on *Dixie Chicken*.

Allen Toussaint's 'On Your Way Down' is another of the album's triumphs. Pianist, singer, songwriter and producer Toussaint had been a mainstay of the New Orleans music scene since the 1950s. In the following two decades his involvement with Dr John, The Meters and The Neville Brothers – all critically praised, and highly regarded among their peers – brought Toussaint to the attention of a wide audience of respectful musicians, including George and Van Dyke Parks. Parks covered two Toussaint songs on his *Discover America* album (recorded before *Dixie Chicken*, and with George contributions). 'On Your Way Down' is a cautionary tale about success and failure in the music world, and was the first of several Toussaint songs that George and Little Feat attempted.

Introduced by Payne's faithful New Orleans piano chords, the song sees the rest of the band lock into a restrained, easy groove over which George delivers a dreamily soulful vocal, the best example on the album of his maturing singing style. Interlocking slide guitar overdubs add to the track's smoky, drifting ambience. At five and a half minutes it's the longest song on the album by some distance, but it never outstays its welcome.

GRAFTED SYNTHESISER SOUNDS

From two of the album's best songs, *Dixie Chicken* then moves into a less-successful experiment, George's 'Kiss It Off'. On this oddity Little Feat are augmented by Milt Holland on tablas and, more noticeably, Malcolm Cecil on synthesiser. Cecil is best known for his pioneering synth work with Stevie Wonder. The brooding, ominous textures that he and Payne build up dominate an arrangement founded on a funereal percussion pattern. It was no doubt intended as an envelope-pushing sonic exploration, but ends up at best an anomaly, at worst something of a gimmick.

This was a time when cheaper monophonic synthesisers were just becoming widely available, but the possibilities they offered were rarely integrated smoothly into bands of the time, most of whom had been honing their sound with traditional rock instrumentation for some years. Instead, there was a strong tendency for synths to be used almost as novelty toys, their bleeps, bubbles and swoops often grafted uncomfortably on to a guitar-bass-drums backing. 'Kiss it Off' is an example of this tendency. Add to that the fact that the song itself is not particularly distinguished, and that George's vocal sounds strained and uncomfortable, and the result is unsatisfactory.

Fred Tackett's 'Fool Yourself' commences side two of the original vinyl issue, and is much better – comfortable and relaxed, in a warm-hearted, melodious, country-soul vein. It starts as so many Little Feat's songs do, with a shuffling Hayward drum pattern overlaid by Payne's chords. The band quickly settle into one of their easy-going grooves, the sort that tended to inspire George to his best soulful singing. This song is no exception in that respect, and the exquisite vocal phrasing sounds like the work of a man at ease with what he is doing. The sessions might have been far from easy, but most of the music that came out of them sounded confident and relaxed.

The next song, 'Walkin' All Night', is the album's sole Payne/Barrère collaboration. It's a medium-paced rocker, similar in tempo and construction to some of George's contributions to the album, including the title track. It shares similar arrangement traits, too: abundant slide guitar, female backing vocals in a singalong chorus, and Payne's propulsive piano rhythms.

The main difference, though, is that George steps back to allow Barrère a chance at the microphone. The resulting vocal, although perfectly adequate, merely confirms that George was the best singer in Little Feat by some distance. It means that the impact of this song, and indeed most Little Feat songs of the period that he didn't sing, is immediately diminished.

The contrast is made even sharper by the next song, George's 'Fat Man In The Bathtub'. Stripped back to its component parts, it has some similarities as a song and arrangement to 'Walkin' All Night'. It's a libidinous medium-paced rocker, with massed harmony vocals on a rousing chorus made for audience participation at concerts, plus slide guitar, neat flick-of-the-wrist rhythm guitar licks, and Payne's piano. In fact 'Fat Man' is not a great melody or a particularly interesting chord progression, but George was able to animate it by stamping it with his personality. He could lift material that might have sounded mediocre in another context to somewhere special through the strength of his vocal performance, thanks to his wit, attitude, feel, soul … call it what you will. Like 'Dixie Chicken' itself, 'Fat Man In The Bathtub' became a live favourite – and, on account of the "fat man" in the title, something of a signature tune for the increasingly portly George.

George's fifth sole songwriting credit on *Dixie Chicken* is 'Juliette', a song that dates back several years. It had been recorded by the first line-up of Little Feat during the pre-Warners sessions in 1969 that had also produced the slow version of 'Teenage Nervous Breakdown'. The *Dixie Chicken* version has a wandering flute part – this was the last time George played the instrument on record – and jazzy electric and acoustic piano chords, plus a bluesy vocal performance by George, making 'Juliette' periodically reminiscent of the softer material that Led Zeppelin produced in the early 1970s. The older recording of the song (with the title spelled 'Juliet') was much faster and was dominated by a guitar part missing from this later take.

After 'Juliette', *Dixie Chicken* slips into the end-of-the-night, party's-over mood of the instrumental 'Lafayette Railroad', providing an understated ending to an album of unpredictable mood swings. Outtakes from *Dixie Chicken* on *Hotcakes* include an early cut of Barrère's 'Hi Roller', at this stage titled 'Ace In The Hole', which would eventually appear on *Time Loves A Hero*, and George and Payne's 'Eldorado Slim', a jazzy instrumental they featured on stage in extended form around this time. Live versions of 'Slim' appear on several live bootlegs from this period as well.

The launch of *Dixie Chicken* in January 1973 saw George make a rare compromise to indulge music business promotional tomfoolery when he agreed to dress up in a chicken suit for visits to radio stations while on tour. Concern about retaining a shred of dignity meant that he drew the line at wearing the suit's head. That particularly dubious honour was foisted on Barrère. George was by this time quite sharp about business matters, and used touring to conduct some informal market research, visiting local record shops to check if the new album was in the racks. If it wasn't – and it often wasn't – George would duly make a note of the name of the local Warners sales rep, and on returning took the list of miscreants to the label's head office and filed a complaint about them. He shouldn't have bothered with the chicken suit, as it didn't achieve much. Most estimates suggest around 35,000 customers found themselves gazing at Neon Parks's blank-faced, silver-haired beauty held in the embrace of an exaggeratedly elongated accordion as they puzzled out Little Feat's new direction on *Dixie Chicken*. It was an improvement on the sales for *Sailin' Shoes* and *Little Feat*, but still a long way from anything like commercial success.

It's important to remember that the status now attached to these first three albums, especially *Dixie Chicken* and *Sailin' Shoes*, was largely acquired through fans who discovered them retrospectively later in the 1970s. It's true that critics received all three albums warmly at the time. Bud Scoppa in *Rolling Stone* perceptively noted a "dense, careening, nearly out-of-control feeling"[15] on *Dixie Chicken*. But those far-sighted critics apart, not many people thought that any of the albums were important at the time.

LITTLE FEAT: CULT HEROES

Little Feat were still unknown to most of the American record-buying public. They were a minor band playing supports and small venues, so unsuccessful that their future seemed perpetually in doubt. Or, to add a more positive spin, they were a cult band. New bassist Gradney, someone working inside the music business who could be expected to know more than most about what was going on, later admitted that he had never even heard of Little Feat when he auditioned for them. In the UK, matters were even worse. Little Feat were revered only among a few enlightened journalists and a small coterie of devoted enthusiasts who had obtained import copies of the first album and then investigated *Sailin' Shoes* and *Dixie Chicken*.

Being a cult hero has little reward, aside from the adulation of a few fans. It is certainly a badly paid occupation. Eventually, the weight of such commercial pressures, alongside burgeoning creative tensions, forced a split in Little Feat. Payne said, "It happened because we had begun to turn on each other creatively."[16] George meanwhile emphasised the financial burdens, saying: "The band for a while was a great hobby, but we weren't able to make it a commercial success."[17]

As usually happened with Little Feat, the facts of the split were reported in different ways, making it all but impossible now to get to the truth of what happened and when. But a kind of consensus does emerge. First, drummer Hayward left briefly, to be replaced for a few months by Freddy White, brother of Earth Wind & Fire's Maurice White. There had been tensions between Hayward and George: the ever vigorous and inventive drummer was reluctant to play the same part twice; George, typically, wanted more control over what was happening. Hayward briefly played with Ike Turner and with Rick Nelson.

A real split between the remaining members did take place, but it was shortlived – maybe no more than a few weeks, and probably in early 1974, although it may have been earlier. The band was inactive for a while afterward as members drifted into all manner of sessions and collaborations, either collectively or individually – as much as anything driven by simple financial necessity. Payne found lucrative work with The Doobie Brothers, although to his credit when offered the opportunity to join permanently he resisted the security that role offered when George reconvened Little Feat for *Feats Don't Fail Me Now* later in 1974.

JOHN CALE AND *PARIS 1919*

George played a number of sessions at this time, including one for the debut of Zappa protégé, Kathy Dalton, which most agree was an undistinguished affair, and another for an album with jazz drummer/bandleader Chico Hamilton. Other members of Little Feat appeared on both these albums. A much more notable collaboration was with John Cale, the maverick Welsh singer, songwriter, pianist, viola player, producer and former member of The Velvet Underground, for his *Paris 1919* album. Cale was in the latter days of an uncomfortable, ill-defined staff role at Warners when he made the record, the undisputed masterpiece of his orchestral pop phase.

George's involvement in *Paris 1919* often goes unnoticed, but when it is pointed out the reaction is usually one of surprise. This is partly because he and the other musicians were not credited on the album sleeve. It is also related to the type of music on the record. Most of George's sessions were on records that are in recognisably American genres, whether folk, LA soft-rock, bluegrass, soul, or any other style. *Paris 1919*, on the other hand, sounds peculiarly British. In fact it was recorded in LA, at Sunwest studios, but if the credit read "recorded at Abbey Road, London" nobody would have been in the least surprised.

The presence of George on the album is announced with a clarion call on slide guitar right at the start of the album's opening track, 'Child's Christmas In Wales'. From there on, with the exception of his multi-layered shrieking slide on the rocky 'Macbeth', most of his playing is devoid of obvious blues-rock influences. Instead, George's contribution is used as part of the complex pastoral orchestrations that dominate the album, especially evident on 'Endless Plain Of Fortune'.

George had proved before that he could comfortably make transitions between different genres. Now, he showed he was also able to adapt to different artists and the unique characteristics they brought from their individual cultural background and training. It says much about his broad grasp of music, his flexibility and his technical ability. Although he had immediately recognisable styles of singing and playing, he was able when required to make these subservient to the needs of the songs and the musicians he was working with.

Paris 1919 is one of the best examples of this. George makes a valuable contribution, but he doesn't dominate by imposing his style. In other words, he doesn't "do a Lowell George". More constructively, his slide-guitar parts add to the whole, an additional layer of melody and harmony in what is already a lush texture of instruments.

Looking back over George's history with the knowledge of what was to come, *Dixie Chicken* seems like a representative album in two ways. First, like *Sailin' Shoes* it was a reasonable expression of where George was heading with his musical ideas at the time. Second, the making of the record encapsulated the characteristics and tensions of his whole career. Defined simply, those characteristics were a desire for control, a sometimes contradictory desire to collaborate, and a questing, restless nature that was never satisfied but always looking forward.

That desire for control prevailed on *Dixie Chicken*. It is the one album on which he was able more or less successfully to balance his various responsibilities as singer, lead guitarist, main songwriter and producer. There were negative consequences to taking on this enormous responsibility – both his health and his relationships with other band members suffered – but he did manage to make this position of dominance work in a way that he never quite managed again.

The consequences of his desire to collaborate and his restlessly creative nature can also be seen in the circumstances surrounding Little Feat at this time. The expanded line-up that George had put together as a means to develop creatively ultimately proved to be his undoing. He needed collaborators – or at least seems to have thought that he needed them – and they had to be of a high standard of musical ability. But he only wanted collaboration up to a point, because he also wanted ultimate control. Yet players as talented as Barrère and Payne were never going to be content with being sidemen to a dominant figure. This was a particular issue for Payne, who'd started in the band as an equal partner. Or so he thought. His songwriting contribution on the first album was substantial, his playing at least as dominant a feature of the band's arrangements as George's. Payne wanted influence and to record his songs; as Barrère grew in confidence, so too did he.

Eventually the collective weight of opinion in the band was to turn against George. There were signs of that already, but it was still a few years away. For now, everyone was concerned with making a living. As late as August 1973, seven months after the release of *Dixie Chicken*, during which time much touring had been undertaken to promote the album, *Rolling Stone* ran a feature headlined: "Little Feat: Still Out There Among The Great Unknown Bands."

CHAPTER 6

If You Like the Sound of Shuffling Feet

"Lowell was a great storyteller. He had an irony-laden story for every occasion."

FEAT ENGINEER GEORGE MASSENBURG

Aﬁer the release of *Dixie Chicken* George was invited to New Orleans to play guitar on British singer Robert Palmer's first solo album, *Sneakin' Sally Through The Alley*. The album included a version of George's 'Sailin' Shoes'. The image of Palmer that comes most readily to mind now is that of a super-smooth lounge lizard, a mildly dissolute sophisticate, and certainly a mainstream music figure. That wasn't how Palmer was thought of in the early 1970s, although the image was beginning to emerge. Rather, he was cast as an earthy white soulman, and one with a history of singing hard-edged R&B and experimental rock with several British bands through the 1960s and into the early 1970s.

George was delighted to be involved in the session as he admired Palmer, particularly his ability to record first-take vocals, and also because The Meters were backing Palmer at the time. This was an

Lowell George and New Orleans master Allen Toussaint

opportunity for George to experience at first hand the New Orleans funk sound with which he had become so enamoured.

Palmer's story became further entwined with that of George as most of Little Feat also backed the British singer on his second album, *Pressure Drop*. That record included another George song, 'Trouble'. Palmer also toured with Little Feat, and later was even fleetingly considered as a replacement for George. *Pressure Drop* was mostly recorded at a Maryland studio, Blue Seas, where Little Feat had decamped to record their fourth album, *Feats Don't Fail Me Now*. The eight-month period that Little Feat spent in the Maryland/Washington DC area in 1974 – recording *Feats Don't Fail Me Now*, working with Palmer and others, and playing live in the area – was the happiest time the band enjoyed in the 1970s. Speaking later, Bill Payne said: "It was the best time of my life ... It felt more like a band."[1]

MAKING *FEATS DON'T FAIL ME NOW*

Although the sales of *Dixie Chicken* had seen a modest improvement over those of *Little Feat* and *Sailin' Shoes*, Warner Bros were still a long way from recouping their investment in Little Feat. Not for the first time, the relationship between band and label was strained. So when their manager Bob Cavallo located the bargain-rate Blue Seas studio in Hunt Valley, Baltimore, George grabbed the opportunity and reconvened the band after their brief split. The block-booking of several months not only gave George and the band the freedom they wanted to work in a less pressurised studio environment without having to watch the clock, it also meant they could deliver an album at comparatively low cost. George felt so at home in the studio that he was in the habit of referring to it as "our studio" in interviews.

Cavallo had found Blue Seas because it was owned by Steve Boone, formerly the bass player in The Lovin' Spoonful, which Cavallo had managed in the 1960s. The house engineer, who had designed the studio's mixing console, was George Massenburg. He became another important person in the affairs of Little Feat and George from this point on. George and Massenburg had met shortly before the recording of the new Little Feat album got underway when George was playing sessions for Mike Auldridge, a dobro instrumentalist. The two struck up a rapport; Massenburg remembers that George probably "saw something in my idiosyncratic style"[2] while George would often credit Massenburg with teaching him a great deal about the technical aspects of recording.

Sessions for *Feats Don't Fail Me Now* took place in the spring and early summer of 1974, until June of that year. Earlier, between January and March, the band had got together with Van Dyke Parks at the Sound Factory studio in Hollywood. These earlier sessions had produced 'Spanish

Moon', a track that would be included on the new album. The rest of the material was recorded at Blue Seas.

Of the Hollywood sessions, George later said, "I asked Van Dyke if he wanted to do [the album], and we got into an enormous argument with Warner Bros, because Van Dyke is famous for his huge budgets. He was going to do more, but we reached a point where we got stuck, and the band broke up for about two weeks."[3] This is interesting because it would appear to indicate that the temporary band-split discussed in the previous chapter occurred some time in the spring of 1974, although other remarks made by George put it toward the end of 1973. Barrère recalls something similar: "We were getting back together to go to Maryland to record *Feats Don' t Fail Me Now*. We had just had one of the many break-ups, and Lowell was trying to put the pieces back together again."[4] Barrère's reference to the "many breakups" probably gets to the heart of the matter. Essentially, in late 1973 and early 1974 Little Feat were on a knife-edge, their future uncertain from week to week.

A related matter that seems clearer is that drummer Richie Hayward's brief departure from the band, also mentioned in the previous chapter, coincided with the Hollywood sessions, because Freddy White is thought to be the drummer on 'Spanish Moon'. But by the time the band turned up at Blue Seas, Hayward had rejoined. The six-piece Little Feat was in action again.

Little Feat's sojourn at Blue Seas was relaxed and productive, probably the most enjoyable album-recording experience the band would have during George's time. This is evident in the result: *Feats Don' t Fail Me Now* is a tangibly "up" record, a party album. But despite the pleasant and productive time the band enjoyed making the record, all concerned knew that if it didn't get them some kind of commercial breakthrough it would most certainly be their last. The origin of the title is disputed, with both Barrère and Parks laying claims, but wherever it came from it was an accurate reflection of the now-or-never mood that prevailed in the Feat camp at the time. Barrère says, "The title was almost literal. If with this record we didn't 'break through the bullshit barrier', in Lowell's terms, then that would be the end of the band. Lowell was not very pleased with record companies and their practices at this point."[5]

Although there were some moves toward a more democratic creative process in Little Feat, *Feats Don' t Fail Me Now* was still dominated by George. Once again he was the producer, and he also sang most of the songs and took most of the guitar solos. He had the lion's share of the songwriting credits as well. Of the nine songs on the album (counting the closing medley as two) George wrote three and co-wrote three (one with Kibbee, one with Kibbee and Barrère, and one with Payne). Of the remaining three songs, Payne and Barrère took a credit apiece on two, and Payne and Hayward shared the other. The album opened with a statement of intent, a musical manifesto, George and Kibbee's 'Rock And Roll Doctor', a slow, lazy, funky groove, all quickfire chord changes and plenty of space between. This is dance music of sorts – if dancing is a languid bar-room sway with a bottle of beer in one hand and a cigarette between the lips. "If you want to feel real nice, just ask the rock'n'roll doctor's advice," sang George while the band stuttered casually behind him. They might not have cared what they looked like on-stage, and so never appeared the coolest band in the world in 1974 – but at times like this they certainly sounded like it.

'Rock And Roll Doctor' was one of the songs George had assembled by editing together several home-recorded cassette demos of musical fragments. He was an inveterate home recorder throughout his career, and had first begun to make his own demos before the recording of the debut *Little Feat* album. For that he used a small portable cassette recorder, but eventually graduated to a four-track reel-to-reel home studio in a converted garage at the home where he settled in the mid 1970s with his family in Topanga, an artist colony in the Santa Monica Mountains, about 25 miles west of Los Angeles. (Examples of George's rough multi-track demos can be heard on the *Hotcakes And Outtakes* collection released in 2000.)

It fell to Payne to make sense of the cassette tape of 'Rock And Roll Doctor' for the rest of the band. His interpretation of the demo's abrupt changes and missing beats, the result of George's tape editing, gives the song much of its character.

Typically, the 'Doctor' that emerged from this process isn't straightforward. There's an "extra" bar in the first chorus that heightens the tension; a second verse divided by a guitar solo; and the rhythm section briefly steps into a chopping reggae beat for parts of one of the guitar solos. And over everything George stretches out brief legato slide lines that sound like they are on the brink of falling off the end of beats and bars. These are all the ingredients of funky mid-period Little Feat, assembled here in definitive form.

The album's second song is one of Payne's own compositions that George particularly liked, 'Oh Atlanta'. As with 'Easy To Slip' from *Sailin' Shoes*, 'Oh Atlanta' was an attempt to write a hit. Payne did this in response to a challenge from George. When the song was released as a single in November 1974 it didn't chart – even though it appeared to have enough in the way of hooks, beat and energy to make it a hit. In fact, like many of George's own apparently straightforward songs, Payne's overt stab at commercial acceptability was far more complex than it first appeared. British critic Adam Sweeting described it as "a riot of modulation".[6] Payne sang the song himself and his piano held the arrangement together, so George's musical contribution was limited to a few slide-guitar embellishments.

Second guitarist Paul Barrère contributed the album's third song, 'Skin It Back', his first sole writing credit on a Little Feat album. Again George stood back from the microphone in favour of the song's composer, concentrating instead on trading rhythmic funky guitar licks with Barrère to good effect. These first three songs of *Feats Don't Fail Me Now* – 'Rock And Roll Doctor', 'Oh Atlanta' and 'Skin It Back' – are as powerful an opening gambit as the band mustered on their albums during the 1970s. Here was a song each by Payne, Barrère and George (with Kibbee), each sung by its writer, and each a strong song that became a live favourite. They were a good advertisement for the emerging spirit of a collective, democratic Little Feat – but a new spirit that would not be fully realised until the next album.

LOWELL GEORGE AND SIX STRINGS

George's guitar contribution to 'Skin It Back' wasn't typical, in that it was one of the few times he played rhythm guitar after Barrère joined Little Feat. But over the rest of the album his by now established slide-guitar style was much in evidence. It was a style dependant not only on the way George played – the notes he chose, and when and where he chose to play them – it was also the product of his guitar sound. His extended "clean" sustain, as opposed to the more distorted type, enabled him to play the elongated, spacious legato lines he favoured. As is the way with all electric guitarists, this sound on which so much of George's style depended was in turn dependent on the equipment he chose to use. Just as his playing technique evolved over several years, so did his guitar and gear.

George's fascination with technology and his constant inquisitiveness about the sonic possibilities of the electric guitar drove him to experiment widely with his guitar and associated equipment. At the time of *Feats Don't Fail Me Now* he was using a Fender Stratocaster guitar. He said he favoured Stratocasters mainly because he found that the intonation, or tuning, high up the neck was more accurate than other guitars he'd used.

He modified his Strat by replacing the treble-position pickup (nearest the bridge) with one from a Fender Telecaster. Previously he had a Gibson P-90 pickup fitted in the bridge position, in common with Ry Cooder who had done the same thing. George and Cooder were probably aiming to get more top-end energy into their sound from these replacements. George went on to fit an Alembic Blaster 20db booster pre-amp in the final guitar he used before he died, to give extra volume and attack as necessary. While he initially played his Strat through Fender and Music Man amplifiers, he also tried a number of other amps before settling in 1976 on a Howard Dumble custom-made Steel String Singer model, with four ten-inch speakers. This he described as having some of the better qualities of Fender Twin Reverbs and Music Man amps, but providing more control. The Dumble was, he said, especially good for overdriven sounds at low volumes.

Experimenting with guitars and amplifiers is not unusual. Most serious electric guitarists do it. And George's guitar tinkering and amp testing were not unusual by the standards of the time. Some of his other experiments, though, were a little more idiosyncratic, most famously his choice of slide. The implement he used was a Sears Craftsmen 11/16 socket wrench, ideally suited to pulling sparkplugs. Surely, here was an appropriate item for a man who first made his name writing trucking songs.

Like most slide guitarists, George used "open tunings", which are different from the guitar's regular tuning and provide a major or minor chord when the open strings are played. For example, a guitar tuned in open G will sound a G major chord if the open strings are struck. Open G is in fact the tuning of choice for many slide players. George, though, favoured the less common open A where the second, third and fourth strings are altered from the guitar's regular tuning (lowest to highest string: E/A/E/A/C-sharp/E), in each case tuned a tone higher than normal. This creates more tension on those strings, and thus contributed to the clean, bright tone of George's playing.

Again in common with most slide guitarists, George favoured a high action (the distance of the strings from the neck) to avoid hitting the slide against the neck and inadvertently fretting notes and/or making unwanted noises. He used flatwound Fender strings.

George's choice of guitar, amp, slide and tuning all contributed to his distinctive sound, but it was his use of compression above all that defined that sound and gave him the means to play his extended melodic lines. Compression is an electronic effect that evens out a variable sound by boosting the level of quiet notes and reducing the level of louder ones. With very heavy compression, the percussive effect when a string is first hit is reduced, instead making the note start softly. Then, as the note naturally decays or fades in volume, the effect of the compression is to counter this, keeping the level of the note up and constant for longer, and thus creating sustain.

Sustain was the holy grail for lead guitarists in the 1970s: extended notes offered all kinds of melodic opportunities and gave a sense of flow to lead-guitar lines. Most guitarists of the period achieved sustain using distortion. George's choice of compression as an alternative means of increasing sustain was unusual. He probably learned about its value for guitar sound when working on *Sailin' Shoes*. The engineer on those sessions, Don Landee, was a pioneer when it came to great compression-assisted guitar sounds, as he'd showed on some of Captain Beefheart's *Clear Spot* album from the same period and would underline later with Eddie Van Halen.

Contemporaries were quick to notice George's adoption of the compressor. John Sebastian says:

"It was certainly what riveted me the first time I heard Little Feat. That compressed-beyond-belief guitar sound!"[7] British slide-guitar expert Bryn Haworth, who was playing in Los Angeles in the early 1970s and saw George in action, says: "He stood out from his contemporaries because he used compression, which gave him a very clean sustain. He was able to play very long melodic lines. Duane Allman was the only other originator at that time, but he used the more classic distortion sound."[8]

Initially, George used a compressor manufactured by a company called Carangella Electronics and designed for use in radio stations. This venerable device is now in the possession of Sebastian. Later in the 1970s, purpose-built guitar compressors became more widely available, and George used an MXR Dyna Comp model that appeared on the market in 1974. Toward the end of his life he also used a Lexicon delay unit to further thicken and elongate his guitar sound.

This combination of technical arrangements gave George the means to weave his largely pre-meditated parts into the fabric of an arrangement, using the guitar to create lines that in other circumstances might be played on horns or keyboards. George's playing depended not on speed and volume, nor improvisation. In that sense he was out of step with the times because most rock guitarists of the period played loud and fast, and jumped at any opportunity to flex musical muscle in improvised solos. George harked back to an earlier age of rock guitarists such as Scotty Moore or Hank Marvin, and pre-empted others who came after him, like Edge of U2 or Peter Buck of REM. All are guitarists for whom technical virtuosity and displays of speed and volume are not the point. They are more concerned with well placed melodic phrases in service of the song.

MORE FROM *FEATS DON'T FAIL ME NOW*

The fourth song on *Feats Don't Fail Me Now*, the George composition 'Down The Road', features a particularly good example of this guitar style. The held-on swoop that introduces the song was a favourite George trick that he used on several Little Feat recordings, but it's the instrumental break starting around the 2:00 mark that is of most interest. Here for more than 40 seconds George's double-tracked guitars exchange phrases and briefly coalesce in harmony – a long solo by his standards. Neither of the two parts are fast, flashy or particularly complex, and neither George nor band move up a gear. The singing stops, the guitar solo starts, runs for 40 seconds and ends, and the singing starts again. It's all nonchalant and understated, and the joins are almost seamless. The guitar solo is a part of the song. Compare this with some of the efforts of the "Southern Boogie" bands like Lynyrd Skynyrd with whom Little Feat are so often mistakenly and lazily included, and George's status as one of the era's unique guitar stylists becomes easier to understand.

'Spanish Moon' had been recorded in Hollywood a few months before the main album sessions, with Van Dyke Parks producing. The dominant arrangement feature of the song is a horn section, courtesy of another Warners band, Tower Of Power. Parks says, "We laid down the basic track. Tower of Power came into LA to do the overdubs, and their arranger did the arrangement free-standing, after brief discussion with me. Both Lowell and I thought that group was the biggest bang out of Frisco town, and these guys were the real deal, musically speaking."[9]

Parks's production gives 'Spanish Moon' a different character to the rest of the album. The simple drum pattern that starts the song sounds double-tracked, the horns are compressed and trebly, and Gordon DeWitty's clavinet is rhythmic and percussive. The result is more layered than on most of *Feats Don't Fail Me Now*. And yet despite these differences the song works well as a part of the album, and indeed is one the highlights. An edited version (shorn of about 20 seconds) appeared as a single in March the following year, 1975.

The sessions during which 'Spanish Moon' was recorded also produced two interesting outtakes that remained unheard for many years, until the *Hotcakes* compilation. First was a very slick, commercial cover of Allen Toussaint's 'Brickyard Blues', a melodic pop-soul work-out that could easily have provided the Feat with that elusive hit single. Again, Tower Of Power add horn parts, Payne excels himself at the piano, and George's comfortable, country-soul vocal pre-empts the style he brought to maturity on his later solo album, *Thanks I'll Eat It Here*.

The second outtake is a version of the album's title track, close in arrangement to the released version but lacking its energy and spark. 'Feats Don't Fail Me Now' was a collaboration between George, Barrère and lyricist "Fred Martin" (Martin Kibbee) and opens side two of the original vinyl issue. Barrère recalls the three working up the song from scratch at George's home, and that it was a "very open"[10] collaboration. At two and a half minutes it's the shortest song on the album, and is yet more good-time funky rock'n'roll, with a singalong refrain of "roll right through the night" that always went down well with concert audiences. Payne hammers the piano, George slides up the strings with his socket wrench, and Barrère dispatches off-the-cuff rhythm parts with a deft flick of the wrist. Along with 'Rock And Roll Doctor' it's definitive funky Little Feat.

After this highpoint the album tails off rather disappointingly with a handful of old songs, although drummer Hayward has said that 'The Fan', which follows 'Feats Don't Fail Me Now', is his favourite Feat song. A noisy Payne/George composition, it certainly gave Hayward plenty of opportunity for percussive aggression and embellishment. The song dates back to the early days of Little Feat and had been tried out, unsuccessfully, during sessions for the first album. By 1974 it had acquired some of the progressive-rock trappings of the period, particularly Payne's swirling organ part that introduces the song and his later synthesiser solo. It's an uncharacteristic song: its overt displays of musicianship and darkly cynical lyrics about a groupie seem misplaced on what is otherwise a warm, good-hearted album.

From that out-of-place track the album moves to its closing moments, a medley of two remakes from *Sailin' Shoes*: George's 'Cold Cold Cold' and Payne and Hayward's 'Tripe Face Boogie'. Both Payne and George felt that the original recordings could be improved upon, and so the band attempted to do so with this studio re-creation of the arrangements they played live at the time. 'Cold Cold Cold' is taken at a much slower pace, sacrificing the tension of the first recording. 'Tripe Face Boogie' skips along nicely, but then so did the original. What the original didn't have, though, was the free-jazz freak-out that intersects the new recording. Judging by the prevalence of synthesisers and pianos, this was probably Payne's idea. The value of a further version of each song is questionable. It's hard not to draw the conclusion that, if Little Feat needed to end *Feats Don' t Fail Me Now* with two songs from a previous album and a recording of a song written four or five years earlier, the band must simply have been running short of good new material at the time.

LOWELL GEORGE THE PRODUCER

That disappointing ending aside, *Feats Don' t Fail Me Now* still sounds like a strong, cohesive album. Most notably, it's a record that reflects the spirit in which it was made: good-humoured, collective, and largely free of rancour. *Dixie Chicken*, George's first production effort for Little Feat, had sounded fine in the end but had been a draining and traumatic process. George's inexperience as a producer had contributed to that difficult process. By the time of *Feats Don' t Fail Me Now* George had learned a few tricks, and with the help of engineer Massenburg presided over a record that not only sounds good but was a comparatively easy recording to make. If a producer is responsible for both the process and the product, it must be regarded as George's most successful production. In fact the boundaries of the producer's role are rarely clear. They depend on the producer, the artists with whom they work, and all of the circumstances – financial, technical and social – surrounding the recording session. It's this vagueness about roles that causes so many artists and producers to fall out during or after recording projects.

In some cases the producer's role is analogous to that of a movie producer: someone who makes things happen, holds the purse strings, and oversees the management of the whole project. In other situations, a producer is more like a movie's director: someone who has a vision of what the finished product should be, and who makes artistic decisions to achieve that, marshalling the talents of all involved to work toward that common goal. Record producers can come into a session armed with charts for the musicians, or might concern themselves with the technical aspects of recording instruments. They can make decisions about arrangements, and they can veto performances as being below par. They can make sure that the studio is booked and that everyone turns up on the right day. They can order pizzas at two in the morning.

As a producer, George tended to be less concerned with the organisational parts of the job. George Massenburg says, "I remember him as mostly a feel kind of guy. I never saw him come in with a chart. He was mostly a great storyteller. He had an irony-laden story for every occasion."[11] Barrère agrees about this accent on feel. "Lowell was concerned mostly with the performance," he says. "He always had good engineers, and he would come up with interesting microphone-placement ideas. But for the most part he just wanted a great basic track, and he would work late into the night on that, on his own."[12]

George also became interested in the technology of recording, and credited Massenburg for helping him find out more about the subject. Massenburg says that when the two sat down together at the beginning of the *Feats Don' t Fail Me Now* sessions, "Lowell knew what he wanted to hear, but didn't know how to get there. He was smart enough about music and technology to know what questions to ask and, given some clues, to extend his imagination."[13]

George affected a nonchalance about production. "The way I work in a studio in terms of production," he said, "is that I usually just let it happen. I waste a little time and sort of stand around and hem and haw and then say, 'Oh, let's go to work.' And when the music eventually gets recorded, it's done on a very spontaneous level. The complexity is then intensified by some [overdubs]."[14] There was certainly a relaxed amiability about George, but to emphasise this at the expense of his driven, perfectionist nature is misleading, particularly when talking about production. George the perfectionist was more apparent in his production work than anywhere else. That was the trait that drove him to spend many hundreds of hours and many long nights alone in the studio, ultimately to the detriment of his health.

In that same interview George described himself as "insouciant and ebullient", a more accurate self-assessment. The ebullience tended to triumph over the insouciance when he was producing his own band. Tret Fure, whose debut album George had produced the previous year, emphasises his relaxed side. "He took time with musicians that came in to play," she says. "He made everyone feel comfortable and easy before they added their special touches."[15] In contrast, during Little Feat recording sessions George was often a dominating presence, and this often caused friction. But during the sessions for *Feats Don' t Fail Me Now* he was able to manage things so that friction was kept to a minimum.

Although Little Feat enjoyed recording *Feats Don't Fail Me Now* and that party spirit persists through much of the music on the album, it is nonetheless in one respect an unrepresentative record. Paradoxically, eclecticism was the unifying theme in Little Feat's music. There was a huge range of musical interests within the band, and everyone shared a desire to feed all of those interests into one unique, oblique, multi-faceted whole. When this happened, the band thrived. Things tended to go wrong when one or more members felt that their interests were not properly accommodated. For *Feats Don't Fail Me Now* the eclecticism was wilfully toned down, partly in recognition that audiences weren't "getting" Little Feat. Payne says: "I began to see that, in a way, we'd been too hip for our own good in the last few years. We were just banging our heads against a wall. So we thought, why don't we just simplify our approach a little?"[16] The spirit of the album was also a reaction to the exhausting endurance test that had been the recording of *Dixie Chicken*. They all just wanted to enjoy themselves. And most of the time they did.

PROMOTING THE NEW RECORD

By late summer of 1974 Little Feat were poised to make some kind of commercial breakthrough. They had a musically direct and more obviously commercial album ready to be released. They had enjoyed several years of critical acclaim in Europe and America. But what they needed, and had not yet been given, was a concerted promotional push from Warners. Managers Bob Cavallo and Joe Ruffalo begged the label to get behind the band. The result was a better co-ordinated campaign. Specifically, copies of the new record were available in local stores as the band rolled into town during a tour, something that had not always happened before.

Feats Don't Fail Me Now was released in October 1974. The now expected Neon Park sleeve-design showed George Washington and Marilyn Monroe huddled suspiciously close on the front seat of a car driving through a mountain pass. A fork of lightning flashes down toward the car from a dark blue sky. The first 10,000 or so customers got some incorrect information on the back sleeve, with two songs listed, 'Long Distance Love' and 'Front Page News', that were not on the album. Warners hastily corrected the error with a re-worded back panel on subsequent sleeves. Both songs would appear on later records: 'Long Distance Love' on *The Last Record Album*; 'Front Page News' on *Hoy-Hoy!* and also in a much revised form on *Down On The Farm*.

Reviewers responded generally positively, although the album's emphasis on upbeat material did not pass unnoticed. Ben Gerson writing for *Rolling Stone* felt that the "perfect tension" between material, performance and production that had been the hallmark of *Sailin' Shoes* and *Dixie Chicken* had slackened.[17] In the UK, *Melody Maker* described Little Feat as the "most underrated band of today" before erroneously comparing them to ZZ Top and Lynyrd Skynyrd. But although the critics might have had slight reservations about this more straightforward Little Feat, the opposite was the case for the record-buying public. The album sold more than 100,000 copies in the few months after release, making number 36 in the American chart and eventually going gold. Finally, after five years and four albums, Little Feat were a chart band.

JOHN SEBASTIAN AND 'FACE OF APPALACHIA'

The success of *Feats Don't Fail Me Now* notwithstanding, 1974 was also a good year for George's collaborations and sessions with other artists. One of the most creatively fruitful was the work George did with John Sebastian that year. Sebastian was living in Los Angeles at the time, and got to know George because the two shared a manager in Bob Cavallo.

As the leader of The Lovin' Spoonful, Sebastian had been one of the most successful American songwriters of the 1960s, and later in the 1970s would enjoy commercial success again. But in 1974 his profile was low; consequently his *Tarzana Kid* album of that year to which George contributed is not well-known. This is a shame because it's one of his most complete collections: organic, rich, and mature. George's main contribution was to co-write 'Face Of Appalachia', the album's key song. Sebastian also included a version of 'Dixie Chicken'. "Lowell was sending me demos occasionally of works in progress," says Sebastian. "He sent me a cassette that had early rehearsal versions of 'Dixie Chicken', and the other side was a home tape with overdubs – a rhythm guitar with incredibly compressed slide guitar and Lowell humming along with it. That was the foundation of 'Face Of Appalachia'."[18] Sebastian added an elegiac lyric inspired by his relationship with his grandfather that was a perfect fit with George's mid-paced country-folk ballad.

Also productive were George's sessions with Dobro player Mike Auldridge, mentioned at the beginning of this chapter. They illustrate how George's enthusiasm both for different styles of music and for other artists' work influenced his own development. Recording with Auldridge gave him first-hand experience of a genre of music – bluegrass – of which so far he'd had little direct experience. The sessions also linked George into an informal community of like-minded souls, a chain of connections that led to more session work and further collaborations.

George's membership of such informally defined musical communities was important to him for many reasons. For a start, it was one way in which he got session work. But there was more to it than that. What often led him into so many of these working relationships was his genuine fascination with other musicians' work. If George came across an artist who he thought was doing something new, good and interesting, the chances are that he would wholeheartedly support and encourage that artist, with a commendable lack of competitiveness. This enthusiasm is one reason why so many former colleagues, friends and collaborators remember him with real warmth. His influence as a catalyst in many careers should not be underestimated. It also led to all kinds of interesting connections between artists who otherwise might never have come into contact with one another.

According to Auldridge, a typical enough circle of connections was generated among the informal group of musicians involved in his album *Blues And Bluegrass*. "Lowell was visiting the Washington DC area at the time, working with Little Feat and hanging out with Linda Ronstadt, who was also working some dates in DC. They came by musician John Starling's house and we all played some music together one night – and ended up in the studio a few days later. I was working on my recording and also with The Seldom Scene on the *Old Train* project at the same time. Linda sang on a few cuts of the Scene's album and sang on a song called 'Bottom Dollar' on my record. Guitarist David Bromberg was also on my recording session, and he and Lowell and I just started playing around with some changes for fun, and the engineer turned on the machine. We were all using slides, with David and Lowell playing bottleneck, of course, and so when we decided to keep the track we called it 'Everybody Slides'."

Auldridge went on to play with George again some years later, on what was probably one of many aborted sessions for George's long-planned solo album. During this, Auldridge says, "In order to 'direct' me Lowell sat on the floor in front of me in the studio while I played against the rhythm tracks. He had to almost lie down on the floor to be in my line of vision."[19] George also played on a Ronstadt album the following year. These connections continued almost to the end of George's life. One of the last projects with which he was involved outside of his own solo album and of Little Feat was the low-key, small-budget John Starling album, *Long Time Gone*, released after George's death.

Another productive relationship that George formed at this time was with Valerie Carter. Carter started out as a member of folk trio Howdy Moon whose sole album was produced by George in 1974. George was also involved in a later Carter solo record that included 'Heartache', a song George had written with Ivan Ulz many years earlier. George had also played on Ulz's one solo album some years earlier. 'Heartache' went on to become a country hit for Suzy Bogguss in the 1990s – before George's original demo of the song, with extra vocals overdubbed by Carter, appeared on a re-release of George's only solo album, *Thanks I' ll Eat It Here*. Here was yet another example of the confluence of connections, contacts, friendships and collaborations that were such an important part of George's career.

George didn't know it at the time, but the comparative success of *Feats Don' t Fail Me Now* marked the great irony of his career. The point at which the band he had put together and steered through three excellent but unsuccessful albums now finally broke through to a bigger audience was also the point at which his hold over that band began to slacken. Why and how this happened will be discussed in later chapters.

Although George continued to be perceived as the leader of Little Feat, his influence within the band would never be as pervasive as it had been to this point. Never again would a Little Feat studio album be so dominated by Lowell George compositions. The band became more democratic, then split into factions, and finally would no longer be George's band in any real sense at all. But in late 1974, of course, nobody knew that any of this was around the corner.

It was a good time for George. In the space of a year, Little Feat had gone from a band teetering on the brink of disbanding to finally selling a respectable number of records. The band at last seemed to have the wholehearted support of Warners. George's session career was thriving and he was taken on for production work by other artists. He had been involved in one of his best songwriting collaborations outside Little Feat. Commercially, things would get better still in the coming years. Artistically, it would never be this good again.

CHAPTER 7

Help Wanted, but Not Enough

"We weren't expecting this. You people are crazy! Why aren't you home in bed?"

LOWELL GEORGE TO AN ECSTATIC SUNDAY-AFTERNOON LONDON CROWD

The package tour variously billed as the Warner Bros Music Show and the All American Concert Tour trailed through Europe in early 1975. It was a big event. Certainly it would be dwarfed if compared to tours undertaken today by acts as big as The Rolling Stones or U2, but judged by the standards of the time it was a considerable undertaking.

The idea was to introduce European audiences to a host of then little-known Warners acts by sending them out as a package supporting a big-name band. The big name was The Doobie Brothers, whose breakthrough album was 1973's *The Captain And Me*, recorded by the Templeman/Landee team who'd worked on *Sailin' Shoes,* and that included the single hits 'Long Train Running' and 'China Grove'. The tour's supporting cast was made up of heavy-rock act Montrose, Graham Central Station, led by ex-Sly Stone bassist Larry Graham, the horn-laden Tower Of Power, the now almost forgotten Bonaroo, and Little Feat. Of the six acts, only Montrose and the Doobies had previously visited Europe. About 130

Audience-eye view of Little Feat at the University of California (Santa Barbara) in August 1975

people made up the touring party, including band members, road crew, lighting and sound engineers, record company promotions staff, and a nebulous collection of friends, family and hangers-on. The cost of the whole venture was put at about half a million dollars. That was big money for the time. Warners hoped it would prove a worthwhile investment.

The show would roll into a town and stay around for a few days, more like a travelling circus than a normal one-stop rock'n'roll tour. Bands would perform on separate bills of two or three acts at a time over consecutive nights. Then the juggernauts and tour buses would be packed up and everyone would move on to the next destination. The first stop of the tour was England, where only two cities were visited: Manchester and London.

The first date of the tour was on Wednesday January 15th at the Free Trade Hall in Manchester. Little Feat topped the bill, supported by Montrose and Tower Of Power. This all took place some 200 miles from London, which then even more than now was the epicentre of the British music business – so the show went largely unreported by the UK music press. One person who did attend was *Zigzag*'s Andy Childs. His account for the magazine dismissed both Montrose and Tower Of Power, but heaped praise on Little Feat. The band played a set that was drawn from all four albums and lasted for just over an hour. It was, he said, "quite magnificent".[1]

Two days later the tour had arrived in London. Childs met George for the first in-depth interview that a member of Little Feat had given to the British press. George was in a relaxed and amiable mood, clearly enjoying the experience. The tape of the conversation reveals him as a man seemingly devoid of a rock star's traditional self-absorption ... which perhaps isn't surprising as at this stage in his career he hardly qualified as a rock star. At the end of the interview George even thanked Childs for the interesting questions.

SUNDAY AFTERNOON AT THE RAINBOW, LONDON

Another two days later, on January 19th, George and Little Feat enacted a little piece of rock history on a cold Sunday afternoon when they made their second and last British appearance of the tour. It was a gig that is still recalled by many as one of the best seen in the country that decade, a show considered so important that people felt compelled to say they had been there, even if they hadn't. To this day, British music journalists and fans of a certain age are almost guaranteed to mention the performance when talking about Little Feat, along the lines of: "Ah, Little Feat, great band ... I saw them at the Rainbow in 1975."

The grandiose old Astoria cinema in Finsbury Park, north London, was from 1971 until 1982 known as the Rainbow Theatre, one of England's best-loved music venues. The cinema had opened back in 1930 as the Finsbury Park Astoria, and throughout most of the 1960s it had hosted regular rock concerts while continuing to screen films. After its final closure as a cinema in 1971 the building was renamed the Rainbow and reopened in November that year as a permanent music venue. Shortly after this it played host to George's former employer, Frank Zappa, an event at which Zappa was assaulted by a fan. The incident put him in a wheelchair for almost a year. George's experiences at the Rainbow would be much happier.

Two Warners concerts were billed for Sunday 19th January. The evening show featured The Doobie Brothers supported by Graham Central Station. Before that, the Doobies performed a matinee, supported by Little Feat. A little-known band playing a support slot to an audience made up almost entirely of people who had never seen them before, on a Sunday afternoon, doesn't seem like a recipe for a classic gig. But by all accounts Little Feat excelled.

To capture the essence of the fabled Rainbow gig at this distance is impossible. Like all great live music events, being there was a large part of it. The atmosphere, although real enough to everyone who experienced it that day, is not a tangible thing that can be relayed in words. No doubt if Warners released the film and sound recordings they apparently made of Little Feat's Sunday afternoon stroll, people would wonder what the fuss had been about. The facts don't tell the whole story, just a part of it. But for what they are worth, the facts are as follows.

Little Feat played what for them seemed like a normal set, and the audience erupted. When the band finished, half the crowd bayed for more, chanting Little Feat's name well into the ensuing performance by the hapless and lacklustre Doobie Brothers. The other half of the audience left the building as Little Feat wandered off stage after two encores (or four, accounts differ). George's response to the crowd was a bashful, "We weren't quite expecting this,"[2] and an amazed, "You people are crazy! It's Sunday afternoon. Why aren't you home in bed?"[3]

To understand why the London audience should react in this way it's necessary to delve into the mind of the well-informed British rock fan (and rock journalist) of the mid 1970s. It was a time when people were looking for new heroes. For the first half of the decade British rock music had been dominated by a few genres. Glam-rock acts like T Rex, Sweet, Slade and David Bowie were all regulars in the singles charts, usually with rousing, melodic, carefully crafted pop-rock songs. By 1975 most of these artists had already peaked and were in decline, or were dissipating their energies in ill-advised attempts to "break" America. Only David Bowie was able to sustain chart action for the rest of the decade and beyond, and this by virtue of constant reinvention to keep pace with changing tastes. But although these acts are fondly remembered, at the time they tended to be seen as pop acts – good fun and OK for teenagers, but a little beneath the serious rock fan. Remember, the previous five years had been the time when the distinction between "pop" and "rock" had become ever more pronounced.

For anyone in Britain looking for more "credible" rock music, there were several possibilities. There was the hard rock of Black Sabbath, Deep Purple and their ilk. There was the progressive rock of acts like Yes, Genesis, and Emerson Lake & Palmer. There were the established bands who had survived the 1960s: The Who, The Rolling Stones, Led Zeppelin. For the sensitive souls there was the option of looking further afield to the West Coast country-rock acts (The Eagles, Poco and others). And there were a few big-selling solo artists such as Rod Stewart and Elton John. These were the names that for the most part dominated the charts and the music papers in early 1975. But there were rumblings of discontent, and questions were being asked, in the press and among earnest fans everywhere. Aren't The Who/the Stones/Led Zeppelin getting a bit stale? What is at the heart of rock'n'roll – individual musical virtuosity or great songs? Whatever happened to teenage rebellion? Does the world need another orchestral concept album? Are tax exiles credible spokesmen for youth culture?

The people asking those questions got their answers a year or so later when The Sex Pistols and the rest of punk rock's first wave emerged snarling and spitting like rabid mongrels from London's art colleges and run-down tower blocks. But prior to that the pub-rock movement had done something to satiate those hungry disaffected souls for whom an Emerson Lake & Palmer live triple-album ("Welcome back my friends, to the show that never ends...") wasn't enough.

Bands such as Brinsley Schwarz, Ducks Deluxe and Dr Feelgood plied their trade mainly on a circuit of small London venues that included pubs like the Hope & Anchor, hence the genre's name. They didn't sell too many records and few sustained lasting careers, but they were briefly looked up to as beacons of authenticity in the period between 1972 to 1976, an antidote to the fat, lazy indulgences of many of the bigger names. Surely this was what rock'n'roll was about? Not some grand gesture with the London Symphony Orchestra, but short, neat, energetic, melodic, soulful songs played live. And if that sounds close to a description of early to mid-period Little Feat, then it becomes clear why the pub-rock fraternity took the American band to heart.

Barney Hoskyns was someone who did actually attend the Rainbow gig rather than say later that he was there. He identified another factor in Little Feat's success that day when he wrote about it nearly 20 years later in *Mojo* magazine.[4] It was, he said, to do with the air of mystery that preceded Little Feat at the time. This in turn bred a sense of elitism among those who "got" what was going on. Little Feat were not like other American bands. There was Neon Parks's enigmatic sleeve designs, George's off-kilter lyricism and humour, and the smouldering blend of art-rock, country-rock and funk. All of this combined to create a sense of anticipation among a relatively small group of people who knew that they were on to something new, something they liked but didn't quite fully grasp, and something that most people hadn't cottoned on to yet. There was a sense of hip knowingness among the Rainbow audience that afternoon, something that always accompanies a band balancing on the cusp between cult status and wider commercial success.

With all that in mind, the response afforded Little Feat at the Rainbow becomes easier to understand. The band filled a gap. There was an audience in London that needed Little Feat, or something like Little Feat. To put it more simply, when Little Feat came to Europe in January 1975, the time was right.

Warners reacted to this rush of adulation by releasing an old song, 'Dixie Chicken', as a single (backed with 'Oh Atlanta'). The single didn't chart, but Little Feat's albums sold respectably in the UK and the rest of Europe from that time on. Most estimates suggest that about half of the band's total sales during this period were in Europe. With a modest European breakthrough to match the modest breakthrough that had been achieved in the US a few months before, things were looking good for Little Feat, commercially at least. On returning home after the Warners tour the band almost immediately started work on a new album, their fifth.

BACK TO LOS ANGELES FOR *THE LAST RECORD ALBUM*

Blue Seas recording studio, in Hunt Valley, Baltimore, had become a home-from-home for Little Feat. Indeed, during the eight months spent the previous year working on *Feats Don' t Fail Me Now* the band had developed a loyal following in the area, particularly in Washington DC which, along with London, became one of two enduring centres of firm support. In Los Angeles, though, Little Feat remained prophets without honour, and the band's sales in the area remained poor. So it must have been with mixed feelings that George and his cohorts were forced to return home to make the LP that would be given the misleading title of *The Last Record Album*.

Blue Seas owner Steve Boone had lost his lease on the building, apparently something to do with people raising concerns about undesirable long-haired types frequenting the studio. The story goes that Boone relocated all of his equipment to a barge in Chesapeake Bay which sank shortly afterward, taking with it George Massenburg's self-designed mixing board and reels of Little Feat tapes. With the loss of Blue Seas, Little Feat had little option but to return west, ending up at The Sound Factory in Hollywood, where they worked on and off for about six months – far longer than anyone would have wished. One positive note in all this was that Massenburg, the Blue Seas engineer, was able to move west as well. He set up his own production company, and worked on the new Little Feat album. Little Feat went into the sessions in bouyant mood: they'd had a happy time recording *Feats Don' t Fail Me Now*; they'd sold some records, at last; and they'd just returned from that triumphant European tour. But simple bad luck and ever-widening cracks in the group's structure all but destroyed the positive ambience. First, drummer Richie Hayward had a serious motorcycle accident that put him out of action for a month or more. His medical bills would adorn the back sleeve of the new album. Second, there were arguments about material and arrangements. Payne felt his ideas were not being taken seriously enough by George. Third, there were worrying signs that George's own creative powers were waning.

All agree that the sessions were hard work, characterised by agonisingly slow progress of the kind that had marred the recording of *Dixie Chicken*. Toward the end, with time running out, mixing sessions ran right though the night. Tempers frayed and health suffered.

Despite the tensions, *The Last Record Album* was eventually finished – and it wasn't the last Little Feat album. The title was reputedly a reference to the 1971 Peter Bogdanovich film *The Last Picture Show* rather than any reference to the band's future. However, rumours about Little Feat's imminent demise had regularly circulated, and the album's title was taken by many as further evidence to back up those rumours.

Warners released *The Last Record Album* in October 1975, 14 months after *Feats Don' t Fail Me Now*. Neon Park designed what many consider to be his definitive Little Feat album sleeve, a nightmarish assemblage of well-known stores, a Hollywood mountain as a giant jelly, and a jackalope (a rabbit with antlers). On the back cover, alongside Hayward's medical bills, George wrote a typical punctuation-free column of credits. The lyrics of the album's eight songs were also printed – including those of Barrère's 'High Roller', even though the song again hadn't made the album. "Maybe next time" was scrawled across them.

The first thing that most reviewers and long-time Little Feat enthusiasts noted was that of the eight songs on the new LP, George wrote just two ('Long Distance Love' and 'Down Below The Borderline') and co-wrote one ('Mercenary Territory'). Of the remaining five, Payne and Barrère had one sole credit each, two songs were Barrère/Payne/Gradney collaborations, and one was written by Payne and Fran Tate (his future wife).

Another change was that Little Feat songs were getting longer. On the first four albums most had been between two-and-a-half and four minutes. On *The Last Record Album* five of the eight songs were between four and six-and-a-half minutes long. This subtle drift upward is significant. It indicates something about the band's changing direction: the tendency to stretch out ever further in instrumental passages.

THE LAST RECORD ALBUM TRACK BY TRACK

The new tendency toward longer pieces isn't immediately apparent. The album's first song, the Barrère/Payne/Gradney collaboration 'Romance Dance', continues in much the same good-time, funky rock'n'roll vein as *Feats Don't Fail Me Now*. George doesn't sing, and his contribution is limited to a few slide-guitar embellishments buried deep in the mix. He has a more significant role in the album's second song, Barrère's 'All That You Dream', which also features a guitar contribution by former Orleans leader John Hall.

With a strong melody elegantly phrased by George, 'Dream' is one of Barrère's best songs, and has become a Little Feat staple over the years. The arrangement, though, was typical of the band's tendency to pull in several directions at once. Previously, one of the great strengths of Little Feat had been the ability to absorb a whole gamut of musical influences into a unique whole. On *The Last Record Album*, and indeed within the three-and-a-half-minutes-plus of this song alone, the assimilation process seems incomplete. The warm, soulful melody of 'All That You Dream' is one of the strongest on the album, but the intricate, cerebral guitar/bass figure that starts the song and reappears with extra jazzy overlays two thirds of the way through sounds like it belongs in another song. Perhaps the band were conscious of this, because when the song was released in abbreviated form as a single some months after the album, work had been done to make the joins between sections sound less conspicuous.

George fans might have been disappointed that so few of his songs appeared on *The Last Record Album*, but at least one of the few was one of his best. The concise country-soul ballad 'Long Distance Love' is a two-minutes-and-43-seconds lesson in all that was great about Lowell George. The lyrics are among his most straightforward and heartfelt, containing only a few of his eccentric tangential twists. In George's world it is not the face nor the eyes of the subject of the song that catches his attention, but her toes. "You know her toes were so pretty," he sings, "and her life so sweet." Likewise the occasional tendency to musical trickery and unnecessary complexity is here kept well under control. Structurally, the song is conventionally assembled: three verses, three choruses, and an instrumental on the chorus chords. The only unusual feature is the stuttering "extra" beats that lead into the first and last choruses. Hayward and Gradney's rhythm is stripped back to the bare essentials, and Payne's electric piano flourishes are modest, precise and tasteful.

George used a warmer, mellower guitar tone than usual for his guitar solo on 'Long Distance Love', which British slide guitarist Bryn Haworth rates as the prime example of how he constructed his guitar parts to complement the song.[5] The pleading guitars are the perfect foil to George's vocal, the two components more like parts of a perfectly poised whole than the separate ingredients of an arrangement. Valerie Carter and Fran Tate sing subtle harmonies in the choruses. The result is sometimes reminiscent of early Van Morrison ballads such as 'Crazy Love' from *Moondance*, and glides along with the easy grace of an early Al Green recording.

This sublime moment is followed on *The Last Record Album* by 'Day Or Night', a song that Payne had co-written with Fran Tate. Sung by Payne, and with a heavily keyboard-dominated jazz-rock arrangement, it leaves George with little to do for the song on record, although he pronounced in several contemporary interviews that he liked it. The song, and side one of the album, closes with a false ending: Hayward's drums, overlaid with random synthesiser noise, fade into the distance and then come back again to the foreground, before being joined by other instruments for the real, final, closing fade. It is a neat production trick.

The second side of the LP starts, like the first, with a Barrère/Payne/Gradney song. 'One Love Stand' is another mid-paced rocker with a strong chorus, and an example of how Little Feat's other writers tended to be better served when George sang their songs rather than when they attempted the material themselves. Payne and Barrère are competent as singers, but their voices sound colourless on record compared to George's effortless turns of phrase and honeyed, husky tones. George sings 'One Love Stand' – and contributes a slide solo – and the result is much more satisfying than the other Barrère/Payne/Gradney collaboration, 'Romance Dance', in which he had less of a hand.

George dominates again on his second sole writing credit. The dirty funk of 'Down Below The Borderline' sounds like the basis for a typical TV cop-show theme of the period. Melodically and lyrically it's one of his lesser works, built on one repeated riff that runs through most of the song. But it hits a satisfactory groove. The guitar harmonics and the jazzy melodic twists of the vocal are closer to the style commonly associated with Bill Payne, and indicate that the commonly held polarisation where Payne is the intricate jazzer and George the funky rocker does not tell the whole story. Payne's big ballad 'Somebody's Leavin'' follows, and marks a complete change of style. It is notable for a weird instrumental passage of bass synthesiser drones and backwards tapes of female voices. George's instrumental contribution seems to be limited to a closing guitar solo as the song fades.

The album's parting shot, 'Mercenary Territory', was listed as a Hayward/George composition on the original LP release, with Hayward's contribution musical. By the time the song appeared on the *Hotcakes And Outtakes* compilation in 2000 George's wife, Elizabeth, had been added to the credits. Her contribution was to the song's lyrics, which were both biographical and prophetic. The territory of the title represents the musician's world, with all its strains and joys, and the song is about the struggle to maintain a relationship in that world. George sings: "I've been out here so long dreaming up songs / I'm temporarily qualmless and sinking." He goes on: "I'm devoted for sure but my days are a blur / While your nights turn into my mornings," before deciding: "Fool that I am, I'd do it all over again."

George forms these lyrics in a melody that owes something to Allen Toussaint, while the band sets up a mid-paced groove, in places with staccato reggae chords. There's a standard George guitar solo underpinned by conspicuous Clayton congas. The song, and the album, fades out with George repeating those lines: "Fool that I am, I'd do it all over again."

Outtakes from the sessions later released on *Hotcakes* include Payne's 'Front Page News', which would eventually make *Down On The Farm* in a form revised almost beyond recognition and with George's name added to the credits. Barrère's 'High Roller' was given another run out, having previously been tried out during the *Dixie Chicken* sessions. Judging by the inclusion of its lyrics on the sleeve, it nearly made the final cut this time. It eventually appeared on the next Little Feat album, *Time Loves A Hero*, having gone through many changes. *For The Last Record Album* it was attempted as a sort of mid-paced sleazy funk and shows that Barrère's writing style was often not that far removed from George's.

REACTION TO *THE LAST RECORD ALBUM*

On both sides of the Atlantic, the press response to *The Last Record Album* was generally favourable, with some reservations. The *Rolling Stone* review – which, oddly, didn't appear until nearly three months after the album's release – was equivocal. It sounded a warning note that the instrumental work was "overdone" but praised George's songs and Barrère's 'All That You Dream'.[6] Similarly in the UK, *Melody Maker* found both good and bad points, deciding that the first side of the album was strong but that the second side faltered.[7] Shortlived British magazine *Streetlife* was full of praise, casting the album as a new beginning.[8] Whatever the critics thoughts, record buyers seemed to be getting the message at last. Sales of the *The Last Record Album* continued the modest upward trend started by *Feats Don' t Fail Me Now*. Most estimates agree on a figure around 300,000 copies worldwide.

The big shift marked by *The Last Record Album* was that it was now possible to talk about Little Feat as the vehicle for three dominant band members: Lowell George, Bill Payne and Paul Barrère. That those three people should have such mixed feelings about the album is indicative of the growing tensions between them – or, at least, between George on one side and Payne and Barrère on the other. George said that he was pleased with the production, although he didn't directly comment on whether he would like to have placed more of his own songs on the album. He did say, though, that the new democratic Little Feat was at least partly his doing. "I wish for everyone in the band to step forward," he told one interviewer. "For a long time I was getting a lot of attention, but, for example, Bill Payne is a magnificent musician."[9]

Payne said later that he felt his own material was "dismissed".[10] He described the sessions as tense and difficult, a result of a poor relationship between him and George. Payne now recognises that this was as much to do with his own personality as it was to do with George's.

An interesting feature about Little Feat appeared in *Streetlife* in late 1975. In it, writer Steve Peacock – who had written that favourable album review – sets up an adversarial dynamic between Payne and George, going from one to the other asking what they thought of *The Last Record Album* and how it was made. Journalistic manipulation aside, the results are telling. Payne said, "I don't want to bad-rap the album. I like it. But it wasn't quite what I hoped for, and I had a lot less to do with it than I did with *Feats Don't Fail Me Now* … I had a bit to do with the musical direction, but Lowell was instrumental in the studio direction, and the two did not always coincide."

George, for his part, said, "I felt it was time that Bill made his statement, and I left him all the room I could." Then, when he was told what Payne had previously said about not having enough influence, George responded curtly: "That's where Bill and I disagree completely: he was involved as much as anyone could be."[11] This airing of disagreements and grievances in the press would become ever more pronounced as Payne and George grew further apart over the next few years.

As for Barrère, he recently described the record as "compressed, clean, very pristine, stifled,"[12] and nearer the time referred to incidents when he and Payne criticised George's handling of the project.[13] It is, he pertinently pointed out, a dark album, one in which there is very little of the surreal humour that had contributed so much to Little Feat's identity up to that point.

Little Feat's new democratic approach was hardly a satisfactory, all-embracing one in which everybody gratefully had their say and felt comfortable with their position and influence. Rather, there was tension and nascent strife. Perhaps George felt all right about *The Last Record Album* up to a point, but Payne and Barrère did not. It was unsatisfactory, like many artistic compromises. It was redeemed in part by the crystalline beauty of 'Long Distance Love', but one great song doesn't make a great album.

Six months in the studio working on *The Last Record Album* along with heavy touring commitments had not left George with much time for sessions during 1975. There were brief cameos on Linda Ronstadt's *Prisoner In Disguise* and James Taylor's *Gorilla*. Apart from that,

George's biggest project outside Little Feat was the Tom Jans album *The Eyes Of An Only Child*. Jans made several well-regarded albums in the 1970s, including a duet with Mimi Fariña, sister of Joan Baez. George was credited as Executive Producer of the album. He also played guitar and with Jans co-wrote the first song on the album, 'Gotta Move'. It's a gentle, easy-going country-rock ballad, pleasant enough but not a particularly distinguished addition to the George canon.

Quite what George had to do to justify his Executive Producer role is unclear, but he seems to have been both a mentor and a controlling figure in Jans's career at the time. Jans implied that there was a dispute between him and George because Jans developed his own ideas about the way the album should go, while George, ever dominant in the studio, resented the loss of control.[14] This tension was typical of George, and cropped up in his relationships with many of the musicians he worked with. His interest in other people's work was genuine and unaffected, as George's long-time friend and sometime songwriting partner Martin Kibbee recalls. "Lowell was a great collaborator, or session player," says Kibbee. "If you called him on a date he would find a unique way of contributing to whatever you were working on, and support your ideas any way he could."[15] This is a sentiment echoed by many. But George also liked to control the creative process, and this sometimes led to arguments and terminated projects.

Despite the problems caused by his controlling tendency, George left a benign impression on most of his collaborators after the immediate tensions had receded. That was certainly true of Jans. Speaking in 1977, he said: "Lowell George had a good effect on that album. Lowell is one of the greatest musical spirits that's ever been put on the face of the earth. Really, the guy is a genius – and whatever he goes through in the band and [whatever his] misfortunes, his musical spirit carries him... He gave me an insight into the good way that records can be made."[16]

It was also around this time that George signed a solo deal with Warners. This could have been interpreted as his first step away from the band he had formed, and perhaps it was. But at the time, he took advantage of the deal for the benefit of Little Feat, using the advance as a way of funding further album sessions.

FASHIONS SHIFT IN MID-SEVENTIES ROCK

This year – 1975 – was a pivotal one in George's career. Commercially, Little Feat were in the ascendant, and that trend would continue for a few more years. Audiences loved them. And for a while longer the band could continue to bathe in the glow of several years of accumulated critical adulation. But that did not last. Critical adulation, along with the respect of other musicians, had been important to Little Feat. Although not sufficient in itself to sustain them through the lean years, it had provided some sustenance and encouragement. It had also become something integral to the group's identity, or at least how the group was perceived. The phrase "critic's favourites" became virtually an addendum to the band's name. But times were changing, and within a few short years the critics' focus would shift. *New Musical Express* of November 8th 1975 published a glowing review of *The Last Record Album*. In the same issue an article by a young writer, Charles Shaar Murray, headlined "Are You Alive To The Jive Of The Sounds Of 75" focussed on the emerging New York punk scene of The Ramones, Blondie, and Television. Then as now, musical trends changed quickly.

Had George remained in control of his band and his creative instincts, and had Little Feat continued on the course they had charted from 1969 to 1974, that imminent seismic shift in taste might not have mattered so much in the long run. The many virtues of Little Feat's music might well have been recognised by critics again, even if the band went out of fashion for a while. But Little Feat turned into a very different band over the next few years. George had started 1975 leading what was probably the most critically acclaimed band in the world. For all its individual musical expertise, the band had a finger firmly on rock'n'roll's pulse. They had a reputation based on neat, short, sharp songs. Furthermore, they'd just started to sell records. Yet by the end of that year it was clear to insiders that the balance of creative power within that band had changed.

George's artistic energy declined and, crucially, his ability to write great songs seemed to have greatly diminished. Within another year, Lowell George would no longer be the leader of Little Feat in any real sense at all. At the same time, Payne and Barrère were growing in confidence. Payne in particular, an immensely gifted player, leaned toward a style that made space for soloing and technical excellence. This emphasis on individual musical expertise – previously held in balance by George's humour, discipline, songs and style – became ever more dominant. With perverse if unintentional bad timing, Little Feat drifted ever further from concise songwriting into displays of virtuosity, just at the point when critical and public tastes started to shift the other way.

The loss of critical support was not abrupt or even total. It was a gradual tendency spread over a few years, and had not gained real force yet. But eventually critical support would no longer be automatic, no longer a given – and remember that for a while journalists had praised Little Feat almost as a reflex action. This change must have been a blow to morale at a time when everything seemed like a struggle anyway. When musicians claim not to worry about what critics say about them they are almost always being dishonest with themselves. Good reviews are encouraging; bad reviews hurt. And for Little Feat the looming loss of press support must have further weakened the foundations of a group damaged by factionalism and by a loss of clarity about their own direction.

CHAPTER 8

Only Time Will Tell

"Lowell had a strange way of showing things. He wanted us to do more, and yet he wanted all control."

PAUL BARRÈRE, LITTLE FEAT

After the compromise of *The Last Record Album* a cloud settled on George's career that would lift only intermittently in his last years. There would be a few more great songs, more luminous guitar playing, and even the best singing of his life, but the fire now flickered sporadically. Too often he seemed abstracted and tired, on stage as well as off, and many of his recordings lacked the crystalline detail, the sharp focus and the subtly internalised influences that characterise his best work. There is an unavoidable sense of a man in decline.

Tellingly, it was often the work he did outside the confines of Little Feat at this time that seemed to engage him the most. "Lowell was always so curious about anybody and their music and what they were up to,"[1] says Valerie Carter, George's friend and sometime collaborator. (She was another who, like John Sebastian, had been introduced to George by manager Bob Cavallo.) It's a sentiment echoed

Guests 1977 (L-R): Bonnie Raitt, Paul Barrère, Emmylou Harris, Lowell George, Jesse Winchester

by many, and is one reason why George formed so many networks of relationships with other musicians where he would play the role of mentor and catalyst. Carter was a part of such a network, along with singer-songwriter Jackson Browne. Both Browne and Carter have said how much they admired George and how much they learned from him. When Carter toured the UK in support of The Eagles in 1977, she said of George: "He's just a great inspiration to me."[2]

George and Carter had started working together in 1974 when he produced the only album by her band, Howdy Moon (see chapter 6). He became involved in Carter's first solo album, *Just A Stone's Throw Away* (1977), contributing four co-written songs, and co-producing two. She went on to sing with Jackson Browne, and the three of them – George, Carter and Browne – wrote together. Browne and George also collaborated from time to time, although there is limited recorded evidence of this. The two had even briefly considered forming a band together, but this came to nothing. The only released example of the pair's work is George's contribution (on slide guitar and backing vocals) to 'Your Bright Baby Blues' on Browne's 1976 album *The Pretender*.

Another notable session appearance around this time was on the eponymous debut album by Kate & Anna McGarrigle (1975), which made the top ten of countless critics' polls, including 'Album Of The Year' in *Melody Maker* and *Stereo Review*, and second place in *The New York Times*. George's contributions are subtle but effective, another of his almost clandestine appearances on a classic album.

FEAT DISCORD

Little Feat didn't have an album to promote in 1976. Apart from session work, George's time was mainly taken up touring with the band and then recording the follow-up to 1975's *The Last Record Album*. The band visited Europe again during the summer, playing some support shows with The Who, including one at Charlton Athletic football stadium in London. When *Zigzag* magazine caught up with George shortly after this event he was ensconced in a hotel room surrounded by recording equipment, editing a tape of the show for broadcast on a London radio station, Capital. That tape is now believed lost. Capital, in common with many radio and television companies of the time, was not in the habit of retaining archive material.

Rumours reached *Zigzag* that all was not well in the Little Feat camp, that George was increasingly detached from the other members. An "odd feeling" was perceived at gigs.[3] But George played down any rumours of discontent, and on the surface Little Feat managed to give the impression of a band riding on waves of both critical and commercial success. The idea of Little Feat gigs not feeling "right" says a great deal about the nature of the band's live performances.

Their show was not one that depended on stunts, props and athletic on-stage manoeuvres, although there were lights and maybe a backdrop. It was not a show designed for stadiums, but one that worked best in smaller venues.

The impression was of musicians at work rather than stars performing. Payne would usually stand to one side, facing across the stage over his keyboards. Barrère, George, Gradney and Clayton formed a ragged and uneven frontline while Hayward flailed energetically at the back. There was little attention to sartorial detail. Mostly the band relied on its playing and songs to grab an audience's attention, and this meant that if the band played well then audiences were electrified. But playing well largely depended on good communication between members, so when relationships deteriorated, Little Feat performances often suffered. Audiences noticed this, because there was little visual interest to distract them from concentrating on the music.

By the time Little Feat's sixth album, *Time Loves A Hero*, was released in 1977 it was no longer possible to pretend that all was well. Reviews, interviews and features in the music press were dominated by several themes. First, there was the band's change in direction: away from rootsy, funky rock'n'roll toward polished, slick jazz-rock. Second, George had a diminished role in the band, evidenced by the dearth of his songs on the album and the recall of producer Ted Templeman. Third, there were now obvious tensions between George and other members of the band, particularly Bill Payne. These tensions had been building for years, and had actually caused significant problems through most of 1976, but as no album was released that year and press attention was correspondingly limited, their true import was not recognised. But by the summer of 1977 George was refusing to speak to the press, and seasoned Feat watchers noticed that he was withdrawn and sometimes irritable on stage, often getting through shows with the bare minimum of effort. It was now clear to many onlookers that something was wrong.

An interpretation reported at the time and that still prevails has Payne wanting the band to go further toward jazz-fusion and persuading everyone apart from George that this was a good idea. In particular, according to this interpretation, Payne and Barrère formed an axis against George and overruled him. George was appalled but, in the new democratic Little Feat, no longer had the dominant voice. He was, according to these reports, forced to hand over control of his band to lesser creative talents, and this in turn prompted a career tailspin that he was unable to stop. *Sounds* put it this way: "Sometimes there are moments when [George] and Bill Payne could almost be duelling, their styles their weapons."[4] Payne is today well aware of this prevailing view, having endured accusations based upon it for a quarter of a century. "The bad rap that Paul and I got was that we had shut Lowell out of the process on [*Time Loves A Hero*]," he said in 1996, "that we wrote a bunch of songs and just had Lowell off to the side."[5] Although there is much truth in this, it's an inadequate explanation of all that happened. Reducing eight years of complex personal and artistic dynamics to a simple equation can never convey all that went on. Payne himself must be weary of questions about the subject, but responds patiently to what he may feel is unjustified criticism. These responses may be well rehearsed, but they are worthy of close attention as they shed light on some aspects of what *Rolling Stone* magazine at the time called "Lowell's retreat from Little Feat".[6]

One thing that both Payne and Barrère have said is that, after *Feats Don't Fail Me Now*, George asked them to write more. Barrère said, "He told me at one time that he didn't want all the weight on his shoulders any more. He told me to become more prolific in my writing styles."[7] Payne too recalls George asking that he and Barrère "take more of a stand in the group".[8] This is no doubt true. After all, by temperament George was a collaborator as well as a controller. As Van Dyke Parks puts it, "He took pains to be collaborative, and found occasional joy in it."[9]

Furthermore, George did recognise the abilities of other members of Little Feat. He praised some songs by Payne and Barrère, although he also expressed reservations about others. The problem was that George never found a practical way to balance his opposing tendencies – to control and to collaborate – so any ideas he might have had about Little Feat becoming more democratic were not developed into any sort of workable system. Barrère put it this way: "He did have a strange way of showing things. He wanted us to do more, and yet he wanted all control. He was not an organiser. Little Feat was always under the rule of Lowell, but when it became obvious there were other people in the group, and when Lowell encouraged us, the diplomacy sort of broke down."[10]

Given that George wanted other people to contribute yet also wanted to maintain control, then the fact that Payne and Barrère started writing more is not remarkable. What is remarkable is that their contributions came to dominate in such a short space of time. Why would George allow himself to lose his footing in the band at this time when his instincts as a writer and bandleader had served Little Feat so well up to now? What was it that made him allow the others so much influence when it was primarily his leadership, his vision, that had got the band this far?

Little Feat's new-found success was a lot to do with it, because this meant more touring. When on the road, George was drawn into an ever-widening round of promotional interviews. He was not only the band's lead singer, lead guitarist, main songwriter and producer, he was also the spokesman. Add to that his extra-curricular activities as a session player and producer-for-hire, as well as the continuing sessions for a solo album that started around this time, and the weight of responsibility overwhelmed him. He was doing too much. He needed help from his colleagues, and although he may well have had concerns about where this help would lead the band, he had no option but to seek it.

Success also meant that George simply had less time for writing and was no longer able to generate sufficient new material to fill most of an album, which had been his usual level of contribution up to and including *Feats Don' t Fail Me Now*. Additionally, the backlog of material that he and Payne had built up in the band's formative years was now all but exhausted. Meanwhile, Payne and Barrère each had songs they wanted to record, and the reduction in George's output left them the space they wanted.

The much reduced quota of George songs on *The Last Record Album* started a trend that continued on *Time Loves A Hero*, with the contribution of the erstwhile songwriting mainstay reduced still further to one sole credit and one co-credit. There were rumours that George was keeping a cache of new songs back for his solo album in progress, rumours that were scotched when that album eventually appeared two years later. Payne claims that Little Feat recorded every song George put up for consideration at this time, and that the charge that he and Barrère were rejecting George's material is unjustified. In the absence of a posthumously discovered cache of lost George songs, that claim seems justified.

The last part of Payne's "defence" is that George's health was failing. He was, says Payne, neither physically nor psychologically capable of dominating the whole process of making an album as he had done previously, or even of continuing to lead the band. This particularly applied to the sustained effort needed to produce a record, which in George's case always involved many sleepless nights alone at the mixing board. Payne and Barrère stepped in and took control because they had to do so if the band was to continue to function. Little Feat had not long broken through to moderate commercial success after years of struggle, and it is understandable that Payne and Barrère – and no doubt the other band members as well – should want to maintain the momentum. This, they felt, was not possible with George at the helm.

George was drinking heavily and consuming large amounts of cocaine, excesses symptomatic of the stress he was under as well as simple hedonism. His sense of judgement seemed to falter. Drummer Hayward said, "The drugs and drink had a lot to do with Lowell's losing his authority within the band … He was very scattered. He'd hide in the studio for days on end, not being very productive, and it made him terribly unhappy."[11] John Sebastian thinks that George's drug use particularly damaged his qualities as a producer, a role that demands the ability to strike a balance between attention to detail and detached decision-making. Sebastian says, "Production was delightful to him, but it's another part of the musical world that gets attenuated with drug use.

Coke does put you chasing your own tail a little, so if you're in the studio you start to get frustrated about a performance that might in fact be great. I think this thing he tremendously enjoyed doing was being affected by the drugs."[12] Another friend, Three Dog Night singer Danny Hutton, agrees. "I remember going into the studio when he was mixing one of the albums, and he was just never happy. He wanted to remix it and remix it – he was a real perfectionist. Cocaine will do that for you. You just start focussing on a little tiny thing and just go on and on and on."[13]

The abuse was bound to take a toll. George contracted hepatitis and was hospitalised for a period in 1976. His temporary absence was a major factor in spurring Barrère and Payne to ask Ted Templeman, who had last worked on *Sailin' Shoes*, to produce *Time Loves A Hero*. The two went to Warners for a meeting with the producer and Warners executive Lenny Waronker to propose that Templeman should help out. Waronker was initially reluctant, tending toward the view held by many that George was the heart and soul of Little Feat, but he eventually agreed. Short of leaving the band, a step he wasn't willing to take, George had no option but to go along with the decision.

Although what Payne says about George's diminished profile in Little Feat is a valid counterbalance to the widely circulated story that he and Barrère wrested control from George, more still needs to be said to illuminate this rather dark period of the band's life. Payne did want more influence, and had been aggrieved by the way in which he perceived George was responding to his ideas. He wanted more of a say, and he felt he deserved it. Although to this day Payne will say that George was undoubtedly the leader of Little Feat, he is always quick to point out that Little Feat was, or should have been, a band like The Rolling Stones.

It was never meant to be a star with a backing group, like Bruce Springsteen & The E-Street Band. It was not a group of musicians under the command of a leader, but a community of creative people, with some more dominant than others, but each with a role and voice. Yet for a while many people thought that Lowell George and Little Feat were all but synonymous, so powerful and overarching a presence had George become. And this must have rankled with Payne. Considered from another viewpoint, it's possible to see the idea of George's waning influence in the band as a misrepresentation of the real situation. Rather, what happened was that George, the ever-creative, restless, searching spirit, wilfully distanced himself from the proceedings. After years of striving to guide his band toward some sort of commercial success, he was looking for something else. It was an abdication rather than a deposition. Lowell's wife Elizabeth George and his friend Martin Kibbee talk along these lines today. Elizabeth says, "This was a period when he was pulling back and evaluating whether he wanted to continue or not."[14] Kibbee goes further, saying, "Lowell simply left those boys behind."[15]

Whatever was going through George's mind, ambivalence about Little Feat took root at this time and remained in place until the end of his life. He seemed dissatisfied with what was happening much of the time, but was unwilling to cut free completely. This was one moment when he might very well have gone off on his own, but chose not to. In the words of Van Dyke Parks, "He was perched to fly, but hesitated. It was then that the whole brood flew the coop."[16] A lingering attachment always remained, even in the days immediately before George's death when the band had split anyway.

JAZZ THING / ROCK THING

The last thing to say about the split between Payne and George is that to portray the conflict as one purely about musical differences is misleading. It was never simply Payne the jazzer versus George the rock'n'roller. Such a notion does not do justice to the breadth of the tastes of both men. Kibbee remembers how George in his youth was interested in jazz, and that this persisted into adulthood. Recently available studio outtakes such as 'Jazz Thing In 10' and 'Eldorado Slim', which date from the early days of Little Feat, were both co-written by George.

'Jazz Thing In 10' is slick jazz-rock, advanced for its day, featuring an extended, improvised saxophone solo by George, and would not have been out of place on *Time Loves A Hero*. 'Eldorado Slim' is another instrumental, more rock-based but again with undeniable jazz-rock inflections. Similarly, Payne's interests extend way beyond his enthusiasm for the jazz-rock of bands such as Weather Report or Steely Dan.

The split between Payne and George, and between George and Little Feat, must not be reduced to simple cause and effect. There was a tangled mess of tensions, egos, ideas and indulgences that at this distance can be partially explained but never fully unravelled. It's a familiar story – the story of The Byrds, The Beatles, The Beach Boys and countless others. It's the story of too many creative personalities in too confined a space, of people dominating and causing jealousies, of uneasy compromises and finely balanced personal dynamics. And the tensions were not just between Payne and George. George and Hayward often clashed too, as did Barrère and George. But one outcome was clear. George was no longer the leader of Little Feat.

Time Loves A Hero finally appeared in April 1977, some 18 months after *The Last Record Album* – the longest gap between Little Feat albums so far. It remains the most controversial band record from George's era because the scope of his influence was so tiny compared to previous Little Feat LPs. Barrère was the album's dominant writer, with Payne second and George a distant third. Of the nine songs, George wrote just one ('Rocket In My Pocket') and co-wrote one other with Barrère

('Keepin' Up With The Joneses'). Furthermore, his lead vocal credits were limited to three songs, and his trademark slide guitar appeared just twice. He appeared to have had no hand at all in many of the tracks. George had become a peripheral figure in his own group, something that would have been unthinkable a year or two earlier.

The album was recorded around late 1976 and early 1977 at a number of familiar haunts, including Sunset Sound Recorders in Hollywood and Amigo in North Hollywood. Templeman was assisted by engineer Donn Landee, as on *Sailin' Shoes*. Little Feat were augmented, as they had been before, by Fred Tackett and the Tower Of Power horns, among others.

Like the music on *Time Loves A Hero*, Neon Park's sleeve design had traces of the Little Feat of old, but with much subtracted. The sleeve showed a vista encompassing a city in a valley against a backdrop of mountains, with a statue in the foreground. The strange, unreal quality is there; the nightmarish, surreal humour is not. George's traditional rambling sleevenotes are missing, too.

LISTENING TO *TIME LOVES A HERO*

Time Loves A Hero starts with the appearance, finally, of Barrère's 'Hi Roller' which had been tried out several times for previous albums. Templeman's production is clear and glossy compared to George's efforts with the song, and much of the sweat and dirt that was so integral to earlier Little Feat records has been bleached out. Despite that, the funky R&B groove and gambling imagery recall the recognised Little Feat sound, delaying the sense of new departures that characterise the album as a whole. George sings well, and it seems like business as usual.

All of this changes with the album's title track, second in the running order, written by Payne, Barrère and Gradney. George is nowhere to be heard. There is ensemble singing, backing Payne's low-mixed voice, dominant keyboards, horns from Tower Of Power, and a tricky chord structure. Compared to material on earlier albums, it bears closest resemblance to 'Day Or Night' from *The Last Record Album*.

The title track of *Time Loves A Hero* and the closing track on side one, 'Day At The Dog Races', sum up best the new Little Feat sound. Sandwiched between them is George's sole credit, 'Rocket In My Pocket'. This is the song that sounds most like the Little Feat of the first four albums: it's a mid-paced, shuffling, syncopated, lascivious, humorous rocker in the manner of 'Rock And Roll Doctor', sung by George and with his lead slide guitar sounding at times like a brass instrument. It isn't one of his best songs – it sounds more like an exercise in how to write a Lowell George song than the real thing – but for anyone primarily interested in George it is the best moment on this album by a long way. The contrast between 'Rocket In My Pocket' and the following 'Day At The Dog

Races' is stark and clear. The latter became the focal point for the tensions in Little Feat. It's a lengthy instrumental that showcases the musicianly prowess of five of the band, and had been worked up in rehearsals during George's absence. He took no part in either the writing or the playing. Later when the band played the piece live – and it is a piece more than a song – George would pointedly leave the stage, his departure glossed over with unconvincing banter about him getting on in years and needing a rest. In fact, George was appalled. He felt that 'Day At The Dog Races' was a misguided attempt at Weather Report-style jazz-rock and that it fell well short of the standards set by that group. He made this clear in an interview with Bill Flanagan. "It was embarrassing," said George, "[and] it didn't fit. It made me crazy. [It was] the complete antithesis of everything else Little Feat played. And it approached boredom to the extent that I had to leave. I had to get off-stage and go elsewhere."[17]

George's presence on side two of the LP is felt only on two songs: the cover of Terry Allen's 'New Delhi Freight Train', where he sings and plays slide; and his co-writing credit with Barrère, the unremarkable 'Keepin' Up With The Joneses'. On the other three songs – Barrère's 'Old Folks Boogie' (written with Gabriel Barrère), Payne and Fran Tate's 'Red Streamliner' (another overtly jazz-rock song), and Barrère's acoustic lament 'Missin' You' – George is absent or an irrelevance.

It's not just that George's vocal and guitar contribution to the album is limited. His spirit is missing as well. The humour, the tangential creativity, the musical wit, the rock'n'roll attitude – all are in short supply, and the characteristics of the rest of the band dominate. This makes *Time Loves A Hero* a clean, clever, detached, cerebral album, with an emphasis on excellent individual musicianship. But not a Lowell George album.

Surprisingly, many critics who had previously presented themselves as Lowell George loyalists did not wring their hands in despair at his reduced role on the record. The response to the album in the UK press was ecstatic. The three most influential British publications were *Sounds*, *Melody Maker* and *New Musical Express*, and they lauded the album without reservation. *Melody Maker* declared it "the band's best album to date,"[18] while *Sounds* said it was "cut-to-cut crammed with classics."[19] In some cases, critics came close to turning on George himself while praising the rest of the band, making George the first to feel the effects of the inevitable backlash that awaits all critics' favourites. In the *NME* Max Bell wrote: "Lowell George has all but forsaken his writing chores and it hardly matters," before concluding that "it certainly makes a monkey out of most other records released this year".[20] At home it was much the same story. *Rolling Stone* stated the obvious, saying that *Time Loves A Hero* "is unequivocally not Lowell George's LP," before concluding that such a fact will "begin to seem more and more unimportant".[21] The record-buying public concurred with the critics. The album sold reasonably well in the US, reaching the mid 30s in the chart like its two predecessors. In Britain it became Little Feat's highest charting album ever, the only one to crack the top ten.

George found himself in a curious position. The group he had devotedly, even fanatically nurtured through lean times had finally gained commercial success – in inverse proportion to the extent of his authority over it. Most onlookers still saw him as the figurehead of Little Feat, even though at this time that was a nominal role. The decision-making power lay elsewhere. Yet despite this he welcomed the band's success, even if his response to a lot of the band's new material – material that impressed critics and audiences alike – was somewhere between indifference and contempt. This was typical of the ambivalence George now felt toward Little Feat. Indeed the circumstances surrounding the making of *Time Loves A Hero* may well have been at the root of the ambivalence. He was both baffled and delighted, both pleased and coolly indifferent.

Speaking of this, Van Dyke Parks says: "Lowell was stunned, as I remember, that Little Feat – his invention – gained popularity at the same time as his relaxation of group authority. I know I was stunned. But at the same time he was delighted. He reacted like a kid who got high praise on a test after no preparation."[22] Three Dog Night vocalist Danny Hutton also recalls George's pleasure at Little Feat's success – a pleasure that outweighed any resentment. For the time being at least, George continued to walk with Little Feat.

ELECTRIF LYCANTHROPE AND OTHER BOOTLEGS

Several live albums of the band had been widely available since 1974, but they were all bootlegs. A trade in illicit live recordings had become widespread through rock music in the 1970s, and continues still. All artists of note have been bootlegged, so the simple fact that Little Feat bootlegs were circulated is not of any note. But the illegal albums have found a place in the mythology surrounding George and the band because of a rumour that George himself produced them, or at least had a hand in producing them. This rumour is particularly strong in the UK, where it has been reported as fact, or likely fact, in many magazine articles that have appeared since George's death.

The Little Feat bootlegs were and still are widely available. Speak to somebody who followed the band in the 1970s and the chances are that they will own one or more of the illegal records alongside the band's legitimate output. Esoteric titles like *Electrif Lycanthrope*, *Aurore Backseat*, *Beak Positive* and *Rampant Syncopatio*, some of which first appeared on the prolific and entirely illegal TAKRL label, were big-selling records. Somebody, somewhere appeared to be making a hell of a lot of money – but was it Lowell George?

The original source of the rumours about his involvement appears to be no more than a fleeting allusion made by George during an interview with *New Musical Express* in 1977.[23] The interviewer, Max Bell, had mentioned the proliferation of live bootlegs to George a few days earlier. George told him, "Sure they're good, I helped produce them." As Bell commented, "This could have been solemn leg pulling." Probably this vague, obscure reference would have passed unnoticed if it hadn't been for the surprisingly good sound quality of a few of the bootlegs, and that some of them were packaged in rudimentary sleeves featuring Neon Park designs.

Electrif Lycanthrope arouses the most suspicion that it may have been an inside job both sonically and visually. Judging by the material included, it dates from around the time of *Feats Don't Fail Me Now* in 1974. According to the sleevenotes it was recorded at the wedding of Hugh and Beddie Jardon. The sound quality is good for a bootleg, if a little thin and trebly. It is a recording taken from the live mixing board, quite clear and in rough stereo, rather than from the other (and generally inferior) bootleg source, the hand-held ambient microphone somewhere in the crowd. The Neon Park sleeve design used on the front cover is similar to that which eventually turned up many years later on the double-LP collection *Hoy-Hoy!*. A dog with antlers sits on the shore of a lake, with an erupting volcano in the background. Some foreground details are different from the later, legitimate release: the bootleg has a bell with a cartoon face to the front left of the picture, while the dog would acquire a garland of flowers for *Hoy-Hoy!*.

Most people who were close to George are baffled at the suggestion that he might have been involved in the bootlegs. In the same *NME* interview in which George had dropped his hint, Payne said that he would be angry to find out that George had produced bootlegs. A few months earlier, in the same publication, Barrère had discussed Little Feat bootlegs at length without mentioning the rumour, so he was presumably unaware of it. Elizabeth George says she heard nothing about George's involvement.[24] George's friend Kibbee goes further. "As I recall, Lowell was rather upset about Little Feat bootlegs," he says, "and I can't believe that he 'produced' them in any sense other than perhaps that his production work or tapes were stolen, along with his copyrights."[25]

Only Van Dyke Parks is open to the possibility that George was involved, pointing out that times were hard for much of the decade, and that George would probably not have been too bothered about offending Warners. "He was never a corporate boot licker,"[26] says Parks.

Finding the truth behind these rumours is all but impossible. Those who run bootleg operations such as TAKRL are shady, elusive figures who are hardly likely to discuss their business and reveal their sources. And if George had been involved it would have been in his interests to keep it quiet, for fear of incurring the wrath of his record company and fellow band members. Perhaps the very fact that he said he did produce the records indicates that he didn't, because if he had been involved he would presumably have wanted to divert attention away from the rumours.

On balance it seems likely that George did not produce Little Feat bootlegs. Maybe his remark to the *NME* was a way of having a dig at Payne and Barrère. He was on bad terms with them at the time, and would know that such rumours would annoy them. Maybe he turned a blind eye to someone from the soundcrew who gave live tapes to the bootleggers? Or maybe it was just an aimless passing joke, mythologised by the press? The most likely explanation, though, is Kibbee's – that George's production work was stolen. George mixed live tapes of Little Feat for radio broadcasts whenever possible. It wouldn't have been difficult for an unscrupulous operator to get hold of a decent copy of one of these broadcasts, either by making a good quality recording of the FM broadcast or by developing a contact among the radio station staff. The source of the recording could then be disguised by claiming that it was a recording of a live show other than the one actually broadcast.

Even if George had no involvement at all with the bootlegs, they are important documents of Little Feat live in their prime. There is even a case to be made that they are the truest surviving representation of Little Feat playing live in the 1970s, coming to the listener without overdubs, with mistakes included, and full of verve, fire and aggression. By contrast, the official concert document, *Waiting For Columbus*, was – like many so-called live albums – generously "improved" in the studio after the event by the fastidious George.

OFFICIALLY LIVE: *WAITING FOR COLUMBUS*

The release of *Waiting For Columbus* in 1978 was a predictable career move. The live double-LP was a staple release for rock bands in decline in the 1970s, a means of putting out an apparently substantial product without having to write any new songs or spend months arguing in a studio. In short, it was a stopgap. *Waiting For Columbus* was a worthy stopgap, though, and significant too as the last Little Feat album that George produced in its entirety. It was also a justifiable release as Little Feat were renowned for their excellence on-stage. It appeared in February 1978 less than a year after *Time Loves A Hero* and went on to become the band's biggest seller. It did particularly well at home, reaching number 18, although in the UK it could not match the chart position of *Time Loves A Hero* and peaked at 43.

Several concerts were recorded for the album in August 1977, at London's Rainbow Theatre and then at the Lisner Auditorium in Washington DC. They were wise choices as Little Feat could count on loyal, fanatical audiences at both venues: the Rainbow had been the scene of the triumphant show on the 1975 Warners package tour; and the band had worked regularly in the Washington DC/Maryland area during the eight months they spent there recording *Feats Don' t Fail Me Now* in 1974. The Tower Of Power horns once again made an appearance, and while their contributions had been all but inaudible at the Rainbow concerts, they were pulled up in the mix for the album. Former Rolling Stone guitarist Mick Taylor guests on 'A Apolitical Blues'.

The rest of the band decided that George was able to return to the producer's role, and George Massenburg once again helped out. Neon Park's sleeve – a red woman's body with a tomato for a head, reclining in a hammock – marked a return to garish surreal humour after his restrained illustration for *Time Loves A Hero*. And George once again free-associated the sleeve credits. It was like old times.

George relished getting back to production, and according to Elizabeth George he worked "very hard" on the project.[27] Working hard meant too many long nights without sleep, which was not wise after his recent illness, but he was pleased with the result of his labours. The album's sound is warm and full, with more precise instrumental separation across the stereo spread than many live albums, certainly more so than the Little Feat bootlegs. George's guitar is generally high in the mix, and his singing is excellent – at times reverting to the more aggressive blues holler he used on the first two Little Feat albums. Many witnesses say that the recorded concerts were not the best. The band were still in a downward spiral after the tensions surrounding *Time Loves A Hero* and George was listless and distant, as if his attention was elsewhere. Yet he managed to assemble a good album out of the material at his disposal.

The best live albums often appeal because they contain new or unfamiliar material, or different arrangements of old songs, and capture something of the atmosphere of excitement and interaction between audience and performer. On the first of these criteria *Waiting For Columbus* falls short. There are only two previously unreleased songs, and both are inconsequential. The first is a brief a cappella introduction called 'Join The Band', the other a one-minute run-through of The Fraternity Of Man's 'Don't Bogart That Joint' famous for its appearance as 'Don't Bogart Me' in the film *Easy Rider*. That leaves live "feel" and new arrangements to attract the listener.

The record's live feel is plausible, but Payne said later that although his and the rhythm section's parts were recorded live, many of the guitar parts and some of the vocals were replaced by George during production.

Additionally, one of the songs, 'Mercenary Territory', was not recorded in front of an audience but during a soundcheck. It was common practice to use soundcheck material and to overdub live tapes in the studio, so it would be unfair to say that for those reasons *Waiting For Columbus* isn't really a live album. Nonetheless, it is not a wholly accurate document of the shows that were recorded as its basis.

Most of the familiar songs are rearranged to some extent. 'Dixie Chicken', for example, is stretched out to nine minutes, with appropriate Dixieland horns from Tower Of Power. George makes an impression on two tracks from *Time Loves A Hero* that he wasn't involved with when they were first recorded in the studio, contributing guitar to 'Old Folks Boogie' and 'Time Loves A Hero' itself. 'Sailin' Shoes' is very different from the studio version, recast as a slow, collapsing blues and losing much of its charm in the process. The set closes with a riotous rush through 'Feats Don't Fail Me Now', much faster than the studio version.

For once the press response to *Waiting For Columbus* was not uniformly adulatory. The long-running love affair between Little Feat and the critics was finally coming to an end. In the US, the *Rolling Stone* review by Fred Schruers was descriptive yet noncommittal. In Britain most reviews were negative. *Melody Maker* tartly pointed out that "Feats do fail us now and again".[28] Only Pete Silverton in *Sounds* took a positive stance, hailing the "re-emergence of Little Feat's own Brian Wilson, Lowell George".[29] *NME* was most critical, saying the album "might even be a tombstone" and referring to "the sorry debacle that was the recording of this album at the Rainbow".[30]

That review also characterised the album as "treading water, whilst everyone decides what to do now". Little Feat had finally lost the one thing they could previously have counted on, automatic press support, and relationships in the band were fraught. But encouraging sales of the album temporarily buoyed flagging spirits. What everyone decided to do was to carry on.

CHAPTER 9

20 Million Things To Do

"I never seem to have time to do songwriting any more, at least not the way I'd like to."

LOWELL GEORGE, 1979

I n early 1978, during post-production work on *Waiting For Columbus*, George sustained spinal injuries in a motorcycle accident. He temporarily lost feeling in his left hand, and for the second time in 12 months was hospitalised. It was a bad start to the year – yet in spite of this mishap and his generally poor health he rallied sufficiently to continue with his hectic schedule. After several years of tension and strife, the immediate success of *Waiting For Columbus* briefly raised spirits within Little Feat. The band toured America twice during the year, in March/April and September/October, and started on a new studio record.

George worked on finishing his long-delayed solo album, and was offered the biggest outside production job of his career, with The Grateful Dead. Considered musically, Lowell George and The Grateful Dead ought to have worked well together. George and the long-running San Francisco

Lowell and a heavy weight, late 1970s

psychedelic institution had much in common, being from the same generation and with shared interests in many branches of traditional American music. But the job, which should have provided his chance to jump several rungs up the production ladder, proved to be a disappointment.

By the mid 1970s The Grateful Dead were a very big name, but already an anomaly. They retained the hippie values and anti-establishment spirit of the 1960s but seemed to have lost direction musically. The Dead's 1977 album *Terrapin Station*, produced by Keith Olsen, featured lush horns, strings and backing vocals, which the band thought were overdone. The album that George was called in to work on the following year, *Shakedown Street*, was planned as a back-to-basics set. According to long-time Dead roadie Rock Scully, George was chosen because he was "certifiably funky".[1]

At George's suggestion, a temporary recording studio was set up at the Dead's regular rehearsal space. The idea was to create an environment that would be conducive to relaxed live playing, which George rightly considered to be the band's greatest strength. The mixing gear and outboard equipment were separated from the playing area by makeshift soundproofing constructed from curtains and large cardboard tubes. Backing tracks were recorded live onto two 16-track tape recorders linked together and then augmented with overdubs. Although things started well, the project ran out of steam after a few weeks and George withdrew from the sessions before the album was finished. Explanations for this were not forthcoming, but no doubt George's perfectionism was at odds with the laidback Grateful Dead approach.

Meanwhile, the Little Feat shows on both '78 tours were well received, with critics noticing a newly energised and engaged George, his hands once again firmly on the wheel. It was a welcome contrast to the detached slothfulness all too obvious during the previous year's outings. A review of a Boston show in April said, "His slide guitar was both transcendentally lyrical and mean, while his bluesy vocals resounded with new-found clarity and even some extra grace notes."[2] An October review described George as "clearly the musical force and direction-master behind the band".[3]

The tours also seemed to provide evidence of improved relationships within the band. George would still leave the stage during 'A Day At The Dog Races', but the on-stage banter between him and the others seemed warm enough. During 'Willin'' George introduced Payne as "Bill 'knuckles' Payne" and Barrère as "the other guitar player". Barrère in turn memorably described George as "the Pillsbury Doughboy of rock'n'roll".[4] But any improvement in relationships was a temporary illusion, and before long the old tensions were surfacing again.

One by-product of the Dead sessions was 'Six Feet Of Snow', a song George wrote with the band's keyboard player, Keith Godchaux. It would turn up on the next Little Feat studio album. George's plan for recording this new album, which he was to produce, was along similar lines to the *Shakedown Street* sessions. The Feat record would be made not in a conventional studio, but using a mobile recording facility moved around several different venues, including George's house in Topanga. The sessions for the album were started in late 1978. They would not be finished in George's lifetime.

THE ROOTS OF THE LITTLE FEAT BREAK-UP

Like most once-close relationships that deteriorate and eventually end, the break-up of Little Feat was messy and complicated. The last acts in the drama were played out not in neat, logical sequence but in confusing parallel. George himself didn't really seem to be sure what was going on or what he wanted to happen. Speaking in April 1979 at the time his solo album was released, he was saying both "I'd like to have Little Feat survive a long time"[5] and "I don't know what's happening [with the band]".[6]

There was talk at various times in the ensuing months of George being sacked by the band, or of Payne and Barrère leaving to form a new band. By the time George embarked on a tour to promote his solo album in June 1979 he was saying openly that Little Feat had split, but also mentioning the idea of reforming the band without Payne and Barrère. Two sets of circumstances immediately precipitated this confusion: Payne's dissatisfaction with the way the new Little Feat album, *Down On The Farm*, was progressing, and George's decision to break off work on that record to finish and promote his own solo work.

The backing tracks for *Down On The Farm* were recorded in a room at The Paramount Ranch, an old Western movie "studio ranch" at Agoura Hills, not far from George's Topanga home, west of Los Angeles. The recording equipment was housed in the Wally Heider mobile truck. An arrangement like this was unusual when recording major-label albums at the time, though not particularly radical: The Rolling Stones, for instance, had made records in similar circumstances.

But what troubled Payne was not the way the sessions were set up, but the way they were progressing. He felt that insufficient attention was being given to basic aspects of the recording process like the positioning of microphones – which is ironic considering George's reputation for fastidiousness as a producer.

Payne approached George to ask if he could help with the production, in order to remedy the problems he perceived. He was unequivocally turned down. George, having relinquished control for the band's last studio album *Time Loves A Hero* and then regained it for the live *Waiting For Columbus*, was unwilling to share the leadership role. For his part, Payne had assumed a position of influence in the band's hierarchy in recent years, and did not want to be dislodged. It was a fundamental difference that would not be resolved.

The contract for George's solo album dated back to 1975. He hinted later that he had signed it as a means of getting more money from Warner Bros to finance the insolvent Little Feat. From that time onward the album had hardly seemed like a priority for him – he'd been working on it for several years without it taking precedence over Little Feat projects. Then, suddenly, in the middle of a Little Feat album session, he decided to divert his attention to finishing it. George's decision seemed strange to the others, although Warners may have pushed him into it.

Significant though these events were, by this stage it was obvious that a split was going to happen sooner or later. The final arguments serve as convenient pegs on which to hang explanations, but the real reasons behind the split were deep-rooted and dated back many years. It was about the fight for control, particularly between George and Payne; there were musical differences; George could be unreliable and was in poor health; there was the lack of a clear process for making key band decisions; and they all simply spent too much time together on the tour bus or in the studio. No doubt if relationships had been better then the differences over recording techniques and the scheduling of extra-curricular projects could have been sorted out. But things had gone too far.

LOWELL SOLO: *THANKS I'LL EAT IT HERE*

George's solo album, *Thanks I'll Eat It Here*, finally appeared in April 1979. The title had originally been slated for Little Feat's second album, the one that became *Sailin' Shoes*. The Little Feat connection to the solo record was evident to anyone with even the slightest knowledge of the band's history: *Thanks* had its Neon Park sleeve, the typical Lowell George sleevenotes, and involvement from engineers George Massenburg and Donn Landee.

As George made clear in his inimitable style in those sleevenotes, the album had been made over a period of two and a half years. That was not two and a half years of constant, consistent work, of course, but a host of scattered sessions in many studios, with several engineers and a sizeable proportion of the Los Angeles session community lending a hand. Some impressive names appear among the list of credits, including drummers Jim Keltner and Jeff Porcaro, pianist Nicky Hopkins, bassman Chuck Rainey, vocalist/guitarist JD Souther, and vocalist/slide-player Bonnie Raitt. Bill Payne and Richie Hayward represented Little Feat. Not surprisingly, when the record's release time finally arrived and George settled down in order to write the credits, he couldn't really remember who had played on which particular song.

Neon Park's sleeve presents a stylised portrait of an unusually beardless George wearing what appears to be a blue towelling dressing gown. The portrait has something of cheap religious iconography, or state-sponsored Chinese communist propaganda – a smooth, bland, knowing face with a fixed stare. In the background a small group of characters, including Fidel Castro and Bob Dylan, share a picnic in woodland. Further back still, an angelic figure dips her hand into a stream. It's a mysterious, unsettling collection of images, and what it all means is not clear at all. For once Park's work seems at odds with the music, which for the most part was warm and accessible.

The album's long gestation was partly due to George fitting the sessions around his touring and recording commitments with Little Feat. But it was also a result of his perfectionism. His tendency to repeatedly overdub and rework songs in the studio got out of hand, and he would often work in the studio for days at a time, continuously, without sleep or even a break. No doubt the absence of band members with some influence over him who could restrain this tendency did not help. He was on his own; he could do what he wanted.

Whether being free to indulge this obsessive side of his nature was to the benefit of the music on the album is debatable. Some, including Elizabeth George, think not. "He got off track," she says. "My personal feeling is that with his solo album he lost perspective."[7] Such working practices certainly weren't to the benefit of his health.

Thanks I'll Eat It Here lacks stylistic unity, sometimes seeming more like a compilation of songs from different periods – which in effect it was – rather than a whole, complete work. Side one of the album is predominantly lush, warm, white soul, and side two includes two acoustic ballads, a Mexican-flavoured tune, and an eccentric ditty that sounds like it dates from the 1930s or '40s. It's a strange mix.

For many artists the lack of a consistent style over an album's songs may be unimportant, but it is significant in George's case because one of the great strengths of his best work is that it successfully blends styles into a unique whole. That ability now seemed to have diminished, with George at times merely aping other people's styles, or even parodying them. Ironically, the same problems – a lack of a consistent style and the tendency to copy the styles of other artists – had occurred in the later Little Feat albums, the ones over which George's influence was diminished (*The Last Record Album* and *Time Loves A Hero*).

The problems had arisen on those records because band members were pulling in different directions. In the case of George's solo album, however, there was no obvious reason, unless the record is, as was rumoured, a collection of odds and ends and half-realised experiments that he was persuaded to put out against his better judgement, in order to fulfil his contract. Despite these weaknesses, *Thanks I'll Eat It Here* is still a good record. It's well arranged, well played, and has some strong material. Most noticeably, it is beautifully sung. Yet for all its merits it prompted some raised eyebrows when it appeared. Many people felt not only that the album was inconsistent but that, inexplicably, George was not playing to his strengths.

Those who had been distraught when they'd discovered George's much diminished writing input to recent Little Feat albums were expecting a bonanza of new George songs. Surely the great man had been hoarding his best material for this moment? They were disappointed. Speaking about this to *Rolling Stone*, George said, "I never seem to have the time to do [songwriting] any more, at least not the way I'd like to."[8] Of the nine songs on the album, George wrote one and co-wrote three. Furthermore, his only sole credit was a remake of an old song, 'Two Trains', that had originally been released on *Dixie Chicken*.

George was also widely expected to strongly feature his slide-guitar playing on the album but again he confounded expectations. Only two songs have that instantly recognisable sound in any dominant fashion, although there are slide contributions hiding further back in the mix on two others. This was not quite the same as, say, Eric Clapton making an album without featuring his lead guitar playing, but it was nonetheless a shock to most interested listeners.

LOWELL'S EXCEPTIONAL VOCALS

Reviewers of Little Feat concerts through 1978 noticed a new confidence and command in George's voice. Elizabeth George confirms this. "He did spend a lot of time during that period practising his singing,"[9] she says. It paid off. *Thanks I'll Eat It Here* features George's best recorded singing, the culmination of a development that can be traced back to the first Little Feat album – from a coarse, hard-edged blues holler to controlled, intimate soul phrasing.

So here is Lowell George, guitar hero and songwriting genius, making an album of mainly cover versions and without much evident guitar. It was not the expected treasure trove of new material and beautiful slide playing. But while it might not have been what people wanted and expected, at least it was an album full of exceptional vocal performances.

It is more than anything the work of an interpretative singer. In this respect George achieved his goal for the album. "It was very successful," he said, "in that I was trying to sing and develop a style."[10] In an interview for the launch of the album he mentioned Stevie Wonder, Marvin Gaye and Tony Bennett as the singers he admired.[11] All are known for their elegant phrasing and control, precisely the qualities that George displays in abundance throughout his album. But the solo record isn't just about good singing. George's songwriting output was in decline, and he may not have had enough of his own material to fill a whole album. But he did have one last ace to play in '20 Million Things', the last great Lowell George ballad, buried half way through the second side of *Thanks I'll Eat It Here.*

Credited to George and his young stepson, Jed Levy, '20 Million Things' is country soul, in the manner of 'Long Distance Love'. In the same way as the earlier song, it tugs at the heartstrings like the best of Van Morrison's ballads, mining a rich seam of emotion. Instrumentation consists of interlocking picked acoustic guitars over a rhythm section of bass, drums and piano. George adds subtle, quiet, minimal slide-guitar colouring, the plaintive drawn-out notes mimicking the sound of a lone violin. Over this he sings regretfully of "all the letters never written" and "all the things I've left undone", moving to the declamatory chorus: "All I can do is think about you, with 20 million things to do." The events that followed gave the words an added poignancy.

Allen Toussaint's 'What Do You Want The Girl To Do' was George's choice to open *Thanks I'll Eat It Here*. With massed female backing vocals, a horn section, crisp bass and drums, and a string synth, the arrangement has many of the classic features of 1970s soul. Some vocalists would doubtless find themselves buried under such a weight of instrumentation, but George's effortless performance sits comfortably in the track, always clear and never having to resort to overstatement to make its point.

This establishes a style that prevails for the rest of the first side of the vinyl LP. The horns, the female backing vocals, the tight rhythm section and George's singing are the hallmarks of the sound. His production has both the density and clarity of his best work with Little Feat. Details can be heard despite the complexity of the instrumentation. In that respect, side one of *Thanks* sounds something like a continuation of ideas first aired on *Dixie Chicken*, although the slide guitar doesn't appear until track three. It's a style that has much in common with the contemporary work of Boz Scaggs.

The album's second song, 'Honest Man', is a collaboration between George and Fred Tackett. Tackett had first become publicly involved in George's career during *Dixie Chicken*, to which he contributed a song, but by that time he and George had been friends for years. Tackett was George's main collaborator on the solo record, playing guitar and writing one further song. Also, it was Tackett to whom George turned for help when he wanted to put together a touring band to promote the album. Although not such a good song, 'Honest Man' is in a similar style to the album's opener, and again has horns and female backing vocals well to the fore. The funky reworking of George's old number 'Two Trains' follows. The song's arrangement is more guitar-based than the first two tracks on *Thanks*, and George's slide playing is briefly heard, but apart from that it fits into the style of the album so far. Given that it is a re-recording, and isn't one of George's best songs anyway, it seems like a filler. Side one closes with a brave attempt at the Ann Peebles standard, 'Can't Stand The Rain'. George's version is perfectly respectable, without bringing much new to a familiar song. Again the horns dominate the arrangement, but George does contribute one of the album's two big slide solos.

Side two of *Thanks I'll Eat It Here* opens with 'Cheek To Cheek'. It's credited here to George and Van Dyke Parks, although when it appeared on the Nilsson album *Flash Harry* a year later Martin Kibbee's name had been added. With its unexpected melodic quirks and Mexican instrumentation by Los Companjeros, it marks an abrupt change of style from the slick white soul that prevailed through side one. 'Cheek To Cheek' is an enjoyable song in itself, and is evidence of the breadth of George's musical tastes. He often proclaimed an interest in various forms of what would now be called world music. But standing on its own among songs in different styles, it sounds almost like a novelty number, a parody.

The same could be said about the album's last song, Jimmy Webb's 'Himmler's Ring'. George croons this oddity over instrumentation rooted in the style of 1930s and '40s popular danceband music – eccentric horns, a melancholy violin counter-melody, and yet more female backing vocals. Although no specific credit is given for the arrangement, the influence of Van Dyke Parks can be discerned: 'Himmler's Ring' bears a resemblance to some of the music on his *Discover America* album that George had been involved with. Like 'Cheek To Cheek' it's an entertaining track. But the presence of these two songs, so distant in style from each other and from everything else on the album, underlines the idea that *Thanks I'll Eat It Here* is more a collection of bits and pieces than a unified work.

Between those two strange bookends are three songs, 'Easy Money', '20 Million Things' and 'Find A River'. George had seen the then unknown Rickie Lee Jones performing solo at a tiny venue near his home in Topanga. He was impressed, and decided to cover one of her songs: 'Easy Money'. Partly as a result of his patronage, Jones was introduced to Warners, signed, and was soon making hit records. A few months after the release of *Thanks I'll Eat It Here* she had already made sufficient progress to warrant the much coveted front cover of *Rolling Stone* magazine – the very issue that announced George's death. Here again was George helping to further the career of a female artist, as he had with Tret Fure and Valerie Carter.

'Easy Money' itself is a cool, streetwise tale of lowlife characters pursuing the easy money of the title. George sings the lyrics over a walking bass, and there are horns and female backing vocals again, linking the arrangement more to the style of side one. A short slide solo based on the lead vocal melody intersects the song, the second and last prominent appearance of George's playing on the album.

'Find A River' is an intimate, haunting ballad written by Tackett. The instrumentation is sparse, consisting of acoustic guitar, bass and drums, plus some wandering electric-piano flourishes that sound like they could be the work of Bill Payne. The mood of yearning that pervades '20 Million Things' continues in 'Find A River', and the positioning of the two songs together forms the strongest part of the album – although they are out of keeping with the dominant white-soul style of the record. They hint at what a good introspective, acoustic, singer-songwriter album George could have made if he'd been so inclined.

The impression left by *Thanks I'll Eat It Here* is a patchwork of musical genres, although the impact of this on the listener is reduced by the consistently good singing and the high standard of production. On most of the songs George's love of detail in arrangements is complemented by an ability to retain clarity in the complexity. No doubt engineers Massenburg and Landee assisted in this process. The strength of the singing and production together gives continuity to an album otherwise lacking in stylistic unity.

THANKS I'LL EAT IT HERE: THE REACTION

The record proved to be a low-profile start to a solo career. Its release didn't grab public attention, and it wasn't big news in the press, though this was less to do with the album's shortcomings than a simple matter of timing. Had it appeared a couple of years earlier – maybe a year after George signed the solo contract – things would have been different. Little Feat then were still the critics' favourites, and were just starting to reach a bigger audience. George was on the way up. The appearance of a Lowell George solo album then would have been An Event. But by the time the record appeared he was viewed as a representative of a generation whose time had been and gone, a generation superseded by younger, faster musicians.

In the UK, George's record was released in a week that saw the album charts populated by new-wave names: Blondie, Elvis Costello, The Sex Pistols, The Stranglers, Ian Dury, The Skids. George wasn't reviled in the way that many of his contemporaries were during the purges that followed the outbreak of punk in 1977, but nonetheless he was certainly perceived as a member of the old guard. Also, he had been in artistic decline for a few years anyway. By the time of *Thanks I'll Eat It Here* he had the tired, slightly crumpled demeanour of yesterday's man. The press response to the record reflected this. Reviews were not bad, but generally muted and non-committal. *Sounds* posed the question, "Where's the guitar, Lowell?" and described the album as "a pleasant diversion".[12] The *NME* review was similar in tone, and pondered the lack of original material.[13] Likewise, a short feature in *Rolling Stone* to mark the release noted that the album "isn't exactly the cornucopia of new Lowell George songs that Little Feat fans had been anticipating".[14] The album didn't sell well, and was deleted some years after release. For a while it was almost forgotten. When it appeared later on CD it had acquired an extra track, a demo of the George/Ulz song 'Heartache' with newly added backing vocals by Valerie Carter.

The same *Rolling Stone* piece picked up something of an indifferent attitude from George to his own record. His attention seemed to be more on the possibilities of a Little Feat reunion. This all fed the rumours that George had been pushed into releasing the album by an impatient Warners, that he hadn't really wanted it to come out.

Yet some people close to George say things that give a different impression. Musician Catfish Hodge, a friend of George's, thinks it was one of the albums with which he was most satisfied.[15] Martin Kibbee says, "Lowell felt a tremendous sense of freedom because he'd really become master of his artistic destiny for the first time with *Thanks I'll Eat It Here*."[16] George himself gave the impression that the album was a low-key experiment, a conscious attempt to do something different from Little Feat.

THE LAST DAYS OF LOWELL

Having not worked with a regular set of musicians when making the record, George had to hire a new band when the time came to tour in support of its release. He turned to Fred Tackett for help with this, and Tackett recruited a band of New Orleans musicians that he had worked with before. Apart from guitarists Tackett and George, the band included bass, drums, a horn section, two keyboard players, and backing vocalists. The new group played quieter on stage than Little Feat, and this suited George because he could concentrate on the newly-acquired subtleties and nuances in his singing, confident in the knowledge that he would be heard.

After ten days of rehearsals George and his new band embarked on a small US tour to promote *Thanks I'll Eat It Here*, starting on June 15th 1979. It immediately became clear to audiences that the musical emphasis had shifted from recent Little Feat live performances, away from displays of individual musical skill to tight band arrangements as a platform for George's singing. He played slide guitar, but many of the instrumental solos were taken by one or other of the horn players. The set consisted of a selection of songs from the current album and a handful of old George-penned Little Feat favourites, including 'Fat Man In The Bathtub' and 'Rocket In My Pocket'. George had avoided talking to the press during recent Little Feat tours, but now he willingly embarked on a strenuous round of promotional interviews as his solo tour unfolded. The shows were well received, with George's singing in particular praised by many critics. He seemed to be happy. "With this band," he told one of the many interviewers, "it's more fun than I've had in a long time. I'm getting off on it."[17]

He was particularly pleased with the reviews and audience response to two shows at New York's Bottom Line club. Speaking to writer Robert Palmer of *The New York Times*, he looked enthusiastically to the future, talking about plans for a new solo album, setting up a mobile studio, and how he had more production work in the pipeline.[18]

But amid all the euphoria of a successful tour and a sense of new beginnings and new possibilities, George's weary body was giving out. His weight had increased to around 300 pounds. He had a heavy cold for which he was taking antihistamines, and he was smoking heavily. On top of the rigours of playing live, travelling, and talking to the press, George was partying hard. Speaking to Bill Flanagan during the tour, he said, "I'm foggy. I just finished working 87 hours straight."[19] Flanagan also noted that George was consuming a large amount of cocaine.

On June 28th the tour moved on to a scene of previous triumphs, the Lisner Auditorium in Washington DC. The venue was one of Little Feat's homes-from-home, and the place where a part of *Waiting For Columbus* had been recorded back in 1977. By all accounts George's last gig was a good one. He was wearing his familiar on-stage white overalls, and the happy and sweating George played an energetic 90-minute set. He included a rendition of one of his great songs, 'Roll Um Easy', which he rarely played live. His backing singer Maxine Dixon said she thought it was the best show of the tour.[20]

After the concert George celebrated and gave interviews to the press. The last journalist to leave was freelancer Joanne Ostrow, who recalled that George was speaking proudly of Robert Palmer's favourable review in *The New York Times*. She left at one in the morning. Some time after this George crossed the Potomac river to return to the Marriott Twin Bridges hotel in Arlington. What happened next is unclear, but it seems likely that he spent the rest of the night at a party, or working on a tape for a forthcoming radio broadcast, or a combination of both. He finally retired to bed at about 8.00am.

About two hours later on the morning of July 29th George complained of chest pains and seemed to be having trouble breathing. Elizabeth George summoned the tour's road manager, Gene Vano, who in turn summoned the paramedics. By the time they arrived on the scene George had stopped breathing. He was taken to Arlington hospital but could not be revived, and was pronounced dead shortly after 1.00pm.

In the confusion and shock immediately after George's death, rumours of an overdose circulated. This was inevitable, given that his drug use was widely known. However, the policeman charged with dealing with the scene of the death found no evidence of drug paraphernalia or of drugs having been removed from the scene. An autopsy was called because of George's relatively young age. It revealed that he had died of a massive heart attack.

Whether George's death was caused directly by an overdose or not is an irrelevance. No one disputes that his lifestyle contributed to his untimely death. Dying of a heart attack at 34 is unusual, but an overweight man drinking heavily and smoking is always at risk. Add drug use, too many sleepless nights sitting in front of a mixing board, and yet more sleepless nights socialising, and early death is less of a surprise.

Lowell George's body was cremated in Washington DC on August 2nd. His ashes were flown back to Los Angeles and scattered into the Pacific Ocean from his fishing boat, at a private ceremony attended by his close family.

CHAPTER 10

The Last Record Albums

"Few people can play the guitar that well, and sing that well, and write that well."

DANNY HUTTON (THREE DOG NIGHT) ON LOWELL GEORGE

Lowell George's death in June 1979 was marked by heartfelt and respectful obituaries. There was a commendable lack of the salacious gossip about lifestyles that so often accompanies a rock'n'roll death. George had been a favourite for a generation of music writers and this was reflected in their various efforts to sum up his career.

Richard Williams in *Melody Maker* wrote that "he kept power in reserve and never indulged in pyrotechnical overkill. That's a bluesman's trick."[1] Ben Gerson in *The Boston Phoenix* spoke of "brimming curiousity and steadiness of purpose"[2] while *Rolling Stone*'s Daisann McLane described him as "one of rock'n'roll's most unique sensibilities".[3] David Hepworth in *Sounds* said that Little Feat at their best were "as near as rock'n'roll had ever got to emulating the total, organic motion of great jazz".[4] Friends and colleagues too struggled to come to terms with the loss. Sudden death at 34 is a shock in most circumstances and people close to him were stunned, even though his dangerous

Lowell in pensive mood

lifestyle was not a secret. Some drew scraps of comfort from the fact that he'd been doing the thing he loved, making music, right up until the last. But these were scraps only. As always when a life is interrupted it was hard not to think about all the things left unsaid and undone.

George's passing didn't have the impact of other rock deaths before or since. It didn't define a moment or mark the end of an era in the way that the deaths of Jimi Hendrix, Janis Joplin, Jim Morrison, Sid Vicious, Ian Curtis or Kurt Cobain did. News of George's demise was greeted with sadness and a sense of loss among the wider musical community, including the press and the public, but very quickly attention moved elsewhere. It was left to some of George's close friends and colleagues to make a bigger gesture in his memory.

Payne set to work organising a tribute concert, the proceeds from which would be donated to George's family. Plans for the event were set in motion shortly after George's death, the concert itself taking place less than six weeks later. There was no shortage of old friends and colleagues wanting to take part, and from these Payne assembled a line-up of six main acts: Bonnie Raitt, Jackson Browne, Linda Ronstdat, Emmylou Harris, Nicolette Larson, and the surviving members of Little Feat.

Each would play five or six songs, backed by a house band of Payne, Barrère, drummer Rick Shlosser, Bob Glaub on bass, and Bobby LaKind on percussion. These last three had been earmarked to be members of the band that Barrère and Payne had been planning to form after their departure from Little Feat a few months earlier, a band that in the end never got started. A host of other guests took part, including producer Ted Templeman (who guested with Little Feat, playing percussion), vocalist Michael McDonald from The Doobie Brothers, and the Tower Of Power horn section. Little Feat were also joined for their brief set by long-standing collaborator Fred Tackett on guitar, and Fran Tate on vocals. Only drummer Richie Hayward was absent; he was recovering in hospital from a broken leg sustained in yet another motorcycle accident.

After three weeks of rehearsals, the concert took place on August 4th 1979 at the Los Angeles Forum. An estimated 20,000 people showed up to pay their respects, including the governor of California, Jerry Brown. This was a bigger Los Angeles audience than George had been used to attracting in his lifetime. It was an emotional event, with performers and audience alike shedding many tears. A particularly poignant moment came when an eight-months-pregnant Emmylou Harris duetted with Linda Ronsdat on the old Everly Brothers hit 'Love Hurts'. It was a song Harris had previously sung with that other great loss to American music, Gram Parsons. This was the first occasion she had performed it publicly since Parsons died in 1973. For the finale of the show all the performers assembled for a rousing romp through 'Dixie Chicken', linking arms across the stage for a synchronised high-kick routine before shuffling off into the wings in a snakeline. These antics were in homage to George's on-stage practices. In the glory days of Little Feat he too had taken part in improbably athletic high-kicks with Barrère and Gradney. And in one of his last shows, at the Bottom Line in New York, George had closed the set by leading his musicians off-stage in a sweaty conga, like a displaced New Orleans street band.

COMPLETING *DOWN ON THE FARM*

One of the many things left undone by George's death was the completion of Little Feat's *Down On The Farm* album. The tapes at Topanga were a painful reminder not only of George's death but also the unfinished business of Little Feat. On reviewing these recordings after he had gone, the surviving band members felt that there was enough to warrant an attempt at finishing the album, although much patching up of incomplete takes would be required.

The basic backing tracks had been recorded at the sessions at The Paramount Ranch. These were the sessions that had so disturbed Payne. After that, the mobile studio had been driven to George's home in Topanga where it was set up next to the swimming pool. George then moved to the next stage of the project, working mainly on his own. He taped vocals for all of the songs he was due to sing, six in total, although in some cases these were rough takes. He also recorded some guitar tracks, although these were even less developed than the vocals. In the words of Tackett, "Lowell had done things like put down a first pass on a guitar track, with lots of mistakes and [often] out of time. But he had the idea, he knew what he wanted."[5] It fell to Tackett, Payne and the others to construct a coherent album from these sketches and notes.

It was possible to assemble complete lead vocal tracks for the six songs that George sings, although in some cases this involved dubbing together parts from two or more rough takes. In general the process was successful, although George's singing never reaches the peaks that he achieved on his solo album. At times he sounds overly casual, his off-hand phrasing betraying that he might not have intended the vocals as adequate for release.

Dealing with George's guitar parts was more difficult because most of what he had left on tape was not useable. It was "sketching with tape" as he would have put it. This problem was solved by Tackett and others attempting to extrapolate from these sketches what George might have played, and then duplicating his style to record the "complete" parts in place of the rough takes. To lend the process authenticity, they used George's guitar and amplifier. Noted slide guitarist David Lindley and pedal-steel player Sneaky Pete Kleinow were also called upon to help out, credited as "electric aids" on the album's sleeve credits. The end result of all this is that there is a lot of slide-guitar playing featured on *Down On The Farm*, but little if any of it is actually played by George.

When news emerged that Little Feat were completing one last studio album from fragments dating from George's last months, it was widely expected that the record would be either an incomplete mess or dominated by Payne's jazz-rock material. Neither expectation was realised. Most of the songs harked back to the country and soul influences of early-1970s Little Feat albums, with only two songs of nine linking strongly with the jazz-rock style of *Time Loves A Hero*. Furthermore, you have to look back to *Feats Don't Fail Me Now* (1974) before you find George's name cropping up so frequently in the writers' credits. Of the nine songs on the album, he wrote one and co-wrote four.

DOWN ON THE FARM: AUTHENTIC LITTLE FEAT?

The production of the album was credited to "Lowell George … with a little help from his friends". Payne took the lead role in completing the job after George's death, with Tackett, Barrère and others lending a hand. The result of this collective effort is a clear, polished sound that lacks the density of George's traditional production style and in places sounds unfinished. There are many occasions when one hears spaces and suspects that they might have been filled with overdubs by George. In this way, *Down On The Farm* harks back to the very first Little Feat album. Another feature of the album's overall sound is that Payne was using a palette of current keyboard sounds – enough to lend the album a contemporary ambience when released, but now sounding very much of their time. In contrast, the instruments that Payne often used on earlier records – such as Hammond organ and Fender Rhodes electric piano – are now so firmly established as timeless classics that their appearance does not date a record.

Care was taken to convince everyone that this was an authentic Little Feat album. Neon Park excelled himself with a splendidly grotesque cover star, a bestockinged woman with a duck's bill and pouting lips who sits by a swimming pool painting her nails, while a tiger with a glass of wine lurks in the background. (It had originally been intended to title the album *Duck Lips*.) An attempt was even made to replicate George's rambling style of sleeve credits. Yet despite these efforts, or maybe because of them, painful reminders of George's absence permeate the album. The inner sleeve featured a photo of George, back to camera, walking down a path on his own. And it his voice that can be heard telling a croaking frog to shut up at the very start of the album.

That exchange leads into Barrère's title track (co-written with Gabriel Barrère), a song in convincing Little Feat style. One of Barrère's mid-paced boogies, it boasts one of the album's fullest arrangements and biggest production jobs. It also features the first slide solo of the record. Like most slide work on *Down On The Farm* it doesn't quite sound a finished, perfectly-executed Lowell George solo. Aspects of his style and sound are there, but the tone is thinner, the sustain shorter, and the playing not quite so precise. Whether it's the work of a substitute player or one of George's rough drafts, it's hard to imagine that he would have let it through quality control. That aside, 'Down On The Farm' is a good opener.

The first of George's real contributions to the album is 'Six Feet Of Snow', written with Grateful Dead keyboardsman Keith Godchaux. It's a straightforward up-tempo country song about the loneliness of the road, with one of George's best opening couplets: "Six feet of snow comin' through my radio / It's rainin' in stilettos from here clear down to Mexico." Even bolstered by Sneaky Pete's pedal-steel embellishments, the production is thin and lacks density and warmth. Payne's synthesised faux fiddle is a prime example of one of those keyboard sounds that might have been acceptable judged by the standards of the time but sounds weak in hindsight. George's vocal, like many on the album, is simple, unadorned and straightforward, with a hint of weariness that suits the song.

By contrast, his singing on 'Perfect Imperfection' (Barrère/Tom Snow) is the most fully realised vocal performance on the record and bears comparison with the finest examples of his mature style. A smoky, mid-paced number – one of Barrère's best – it benefits from the space in the arrangement that is a weakness in other parts of the album. Again, the arrangement includes a lot of slide playing, but the same reservations apply. George's only sole writing credit, 'Kokomo', follows. It's a mid-paced, groove-based rocker, and one of his weakest songs, both musically and lyrically. He sings it well enough, but this does not disguise the flimsiness of the material. It fails to capture the attention. Tackett plays slide guitar here, and manages to get something of George's style without ever quite capturing its essence.

From the disappointment of 'Kokomo', side one of the LP closes with the record's best song, Tackett and George's 'Be One Now'. A soulful, mid-paced pop number with a verse of unusual chord changes and a strong hook in the chorus, it is one of George's catchiest, most memorable songs. The production is noticeable for a sparseness that hadn't been heard since *Little Feat*. For the first verse George sings over just acoustic guitar, bass and drums. Keyboards flesh out the sound as the song progresses, but still in a minimal and restrained fashion. The simplicity works well, heightening the poignancy of the lyrics, but it remains a matter of speculation whether George would have chosen such an approach had he lived to finish the song.

Those poignant lyrics came back to haunt the surviving members of Little Feat. Given the strife and dissension that had corrupted the band's last years, it was an emotional experience during the album's various mixing sessions for them to hear George singing lines such as: "Well, I see you so far away / In my memory you will stay," ... and ... "If you wanna love me, wanna be my friend / Be one now, be one now."

Side two of the LP starts on a warm, heartening, up-beat note with a Payne/George song, 'Straight From The Heart'. It was the first the two had written together since the time of *Dixie Chicken* in 1973. George sings to a funky mid-paced pop backing, and the fullness of tone in the slide-guitar playing might just mean that it really is him playing. Another Payne/George collaboration, 'Front Page News', follows. It was based on an old song that Payne had put forward for *Feats Don't Fail Me Now*, recorded at that time but rejected by George, who then extensively reconfigured the song with Payne. That first version would eventually appear a few years later (on *Hoy-Hoy!*). The 'Front Page News' on *Down On The Farm* – the one revamped by George – shares little more than a title and some lyrics with the original version. George sings the song, but the preponderance of smooth, jazzy keyboards connects it back to the style of *Time Loves A Hero*. After 'Front Page News' the album tails off. 'Wake Up Dreaming' is a Bill Payne/Fran Tate collaboration, and 'Feel The Groove' is credited to Sam Clayton and occasional Feat collaborator Gordon DeWitty. George has no involvement in either song.

Given the tense initial sessions for *Down On The Farm* and the way in which it was completed after George's death, the album could have been a debacle. In fact it turned out to be a respectable if modest way to say goodbye to George. And it seemed at the time that it would close the book on the Little Feat story. The album was received with something like relief by most critics; an *NME* reviewer who said "I'd expected a lot less"[6] summed up their sentiments. Public attention by now had been diverted to newer sounds, and sales were down compared to *Waiting For Columbus*.

No one was pretending that the album would not have turned out differently if George had lived. Exactly what it might have sounded like can only be a matter of speculation, of course. Indeed, what George was planning on his return from that last ill-starred tour is uncertain. He seemed to be vacillating between continuing on his own and reforming Little Feat, either with or without Payne and Barrère. The day before he died he phoned three members of the band – Clayton, Gradney and Hayward – to tell them that Little Feat would regroup, and even that he was going to try to sort things out with Payne. Yet just a few days before that he had been telling Robert Palmer of *The New York Times* that he was going to make another solo record, set up a mobile studio, and do some more production work. Probably he didn't know exactly what he was going to do. He was on the road, busy, tired, but enjoying himself, considering all sorts of possibilities for the future without knowing that he didn't have one.

Down On The Farm was released in late November 1979. As the new decade started, the former members of Little Feat scattered, playing sessions, resting, and making solo records. George, meanwhile, was fondly remembered by many fans, friends and family. That might have been the last of Little Feat, but Payne in particular seemed to find it hard to let things go. A year or so after George's death he went to Warners with a proposal for a retrospective Little Feat double album, a last parting gesture, "to give everybody who was interested a little more insight into what this group was about".[7] With the help of George Massenburg and Barrère he began assembling what became *Hoy-Hoy!*.

THE *HOY-HOY!* COLLECTION

Reduced to a list of its component parts *Hoy-Hoy!* doesn't sound that promising: a collection of studio outtakes, live recordings, old album tracks and two new songs, thrown together across four sides of vinyl, and not even presented in chronological order. Yet it is an enormously enjoyable collection. The ragbag of songs supported by written comments from the band and a booklet of assorted lyrics, photos and memorabilia has all the qualities of a good scrapbook – messy, seemingly unplanned, informative, evocative, sad, funny. It's an exceptionally effective aural and visual record of the band's life through the 1970s.

George is absent from three of the album's 19 songs. These are the two newly recorded songs, one by Payne ('Gringo') and one by Barrère ('Over The Edge'), and a live version of 'All That You Dream' recorded at the Lowell George tribute concert and sung by Linda Ronstadt. Those three songs aside, George's singing, playing and writing is much in evidence. His spirit seems to pervade the whole project, from the snatch of a solo demo of 'Rocket In My Pocket' that starts the album to a fully realised, previously unreleased solo song, 'China White', dating from 1978, which appears in the middle of side four. It's a slow blues with massed female backing vocals – and some not especially subtle drug references in the lyrics. Well sung and richly produced, it seems strange that George elected to leave it off *Thanks I'll Eat It Here*.

Other notable tracks include a version of the country standard 'Lonesome Whistle', Hank Williams refracted through the prism of George's imagination. A fiercely funky 'Rock And Roll Doctor' completed with the help of Allen Toussaint is a high point. George lost the master tape for this horn-laden extravaganza on a train, but fortunately it was found some weeks later. An involved live version of 'The Fan' is almost identical to the version that appears on the bootleg *Electrif Lycanthrope*. Most of the rest of the album is made up of old album tracks (three in total), identical to the originals, a handful of previously unavailable live recordings mainly dating from the Lisner shows recorded for *Waiting For Columbus*, and some post-Factory/pre-Little Feat material that covers the same ground as the later *Lightning-Rod Man* compilation (see discography at the back of the book).

Hoy-Hoy! was released in October 1981 to limited attention, particularly in the UK. At home it was a modest chart entry, reaching number 39. It is a pertinent comment on rock music's short memory that the writer who reviewed the collection in *Rolling Stone*, Jon Pareles, felt obliged to use most of his wordcount explaining to the readers who Little Feat had been, and why they were once important.[8]

If *Down On The Farm* was to be the last chapter of the story of Lowell George and Little Feat, then *Hoy-Hoy!* ought to have been its postscript. But thanks to the trend by record companies for repackaging archive material for successive generations, a continuing trickle of releases bearing the names of Little Feat and Lowell George has appeared over the past 20 years. This will continue. Some of these releases are straightforward reissues, but there have been remastered albums on CD with bonus tracks, previously unreleased live collections, and compilations. The most significant of these to date is the *Hotcakes And Outtakes* compilation that appeared in 2000. It has been mentioned throughout this book. A four-CD set celebrating 30 years of Little Feat, it includes one CD of previously unreleased material, most of it featuring George in some capacity. The first two CDs of the collection compile highlights from the band's recording career with George, and include several rare single-only versions of songs. The other disc is devoted to the incarnation of Little Feat that emerged some years after George's death.

REVIVING LITTLE FEAT

Payne instigated this reunion of the surviving original members of Little Feat in the mid 1980s. The gap left by George's death was filled by two new members, the already familiar Fred Tackett on guitar, and singer Craig Fuller. (Fuller had been slated to join Payne and Barrère's aborted new band when they left Little Feat in early 1979.) Many people poured scorn on the idea of a Little Feat without Lowell George, saying that such a notion was virtually a contradiction in terms. Undaunted, Payne and the others signed once more to Warners, recalled Massenburg for production chores and Neon Park for sleeve design, and continued where they had left off.

The new line-up's first album, *Let It Roll*, appeared to a generally warm response in February 1988, charting in the US at 36. Since then the band has experienced fluctuating fortunes, a line-up change, and several moves among record companies. The albums no longer chart, but the band's audience remains loyal and passionate. Little Feat are today established as a venerable institution in American rock, and one that looks set to survive. The benign ghost of Lowell George hovers over the reconstituted band as they play many of his old songs, including 'Willin'', 'Fat Man In The Bathtub', 'Spanish Moon', 'Mercenary Territory' and 'Feats Don't Fail Me Now'. The crowds still love those old songs.

LOWELL'S LEGACY

Apart from Little Feat's ongoing act of remembrance, George's legacy is not that visible. Danny Hutton goes so far as to describe him as a forgotten figure, although this isn't strictly accurate as George is remembered, indeed revered, among surviving musicians of his own generation. But that memory has not been perpetuated to any great extent among successive generations of musicians and music fans.

It is commonplace now for young, newly emerging rock bands to claim as influences all kinds of cult names from the late 1960s and early 1970s. Nick Drake, Tim Buckley, Big Star and The Velvet Underground regularly crop up in this context. They have become familiar with hindsight, yet they sold very few records when active. Why is it that George is rarely included in such lists, given the acclaim he was afforded in his lifetime? As Hutton says, "Few people can play the guitar that well, and sing that well, and write that well."

There are several reasons. First, although George was an underground cult figure for a number of years in the early 1970s, toward the end of his life he no longer qualified for that description. With Little Feat he was making chart albums and selling-out reasonably big venues. Although it would be wrong to suggest that he became completely absorbed into the mainstream, he was going in that direction. And this meant that his cult credentials were compromised. Had Little Feat split up, say, after *Dixie Chicken* and George and the others slipped into obscurity – preferably an obscurity punctuated with personal problems and maybe outlandish religious conversions – then George would be remembered completely differently today.

As it is, if younger musicians and fans chance upon George now they will probably assume he was just another indulgent, long-haired, bearded American rock musician of the 1970s rather than a mysterious and intriguing figure from the past worthy of their attention. It's a lazy assumption, but one that is certainly made, if only unconsciously.

The next reason links to the first. It is that Little Feat had the misfortune to be one of the last critics' favourites before punk rock. This meant that when the new bands started to break through in 1977 there was a tendency to include Little Feat and George with all the other bloated has-beens who were thrown in the cultural trashcan at the time. It was no longer fashionable to like Little Feat and Lowell George. Many lazy assumptions and judgements were made at the time and many good artists were temporarily written out of history. This phenomenon was particularly pronounced in Britain, but to a lesser extent occurred in the US and the rest of the world as well. One impact of this was that a generation of musicians who grew up influenced by punk rock tended to dismiss with a reflex action a whole set of artists from the immediate pre-punk years. When the careers of these younger musicians started to develop in the 1980s and even into the 1990s, they were looking to post-1977 acts or further back to the 1960s for their inspiration. But not, significantly, to the heroes of 1975 and 1976. There are some signs that this is changing now, and many once-derided acts have been critically rehabilitated. The same might yet happen to Lowell George.

In rock-music circles George's continuing influence is confined mainly to musicians of his own generation. Most artists on the 1998 George tribute CD *Rock And Roll Doctor* are contemporaries of his, including Jackson Browne, Randy Newman and Bonnie Raitt. By comparison, tribute albums for the likes of Nick Drake and Tim Buckley have tended to attract younger artists.

Another reason why George's influence is not so widely felt as might be expected is that many of his songs are hard for other artists to cover because of their idiosyncrasies and quirks. Payne says that when the artists involved in the Lowell George tribute concert were preparing for the event they had some difficulty finding George songs that they could sing well because of the complexity of the phrasing. In the end, of the 34 songs performed that night only seven were his. George's generally unconventional phrasing, irregular chord patterns and cryptic humour make the songs hard to learn, interpret and perform. It's as if his personality is so indelibly stamped on the very fabric of his songs that other artists are unable to impose their own identity. It's no accident that his most covered and commercially successful songs are the simple, conventionally structured ones, like 'Willin'' and 'Truck Stop Girl'. In a way, these songs have less of George in them – and that makes them easier to cover.

Another of George's more conventional songs, 'Heartache', became his only big hit when it entered the US country charts many years after his death. 'Heartache' is a traditional-sounding country ballad that he co-wrote with Ivan Ulz in 1971, and it was Suzy Bogguss who in 1993 turned it into a top-20 US country hit. She recorded the song after hearing it on Valerie Carter's mid-1970s album *Just A Stone's Throw Away* that George had been involved with. Speaking about how the song was written, Ulz recalls that he'd had a fight with his girlfriend. "I drove over to Lowell's and his wife was storming out of the house. Lowell handed me a piece of paper with the chorus of 'Heartache' written on it, and he said to me, 'Here, see what you can do with this.' I scratched out a lyric and less than an hour later we had written a song."[9] Although a posthumous hit song is a clear indication of George's influence, there are other examples that are less apparent but equally important. He was much admired by other musicians in the 1970s, and the style he pioneered was an important ingredient of that decade's melting pot of musical ideas. Both The Rolling Stones and Led Zeppelin were known to be Little Feat fans, and Bob Dylan sometimes turned up to Little Feat concerts. Robert Plant saw Little Feat play whenever he could, although few direct traces of this enthusiasm can be heard in Led Zeppelin's music. The same can be said for Dylan. As for the Stones, elements of Little Feat's style can be heard in their mid-1970s output, in the gospel-influenced female backing vocals and the blend of rock, folk, country and soul influences.

But it is among his Los Angeles-based contemporaries that George's legacy is most keenly felt. The list of people who speak of him as an important influence, either as mentor or catalyst or valued collaborator, includes Jackson Browne, Van Dyke Parks, Bonnie Raitt, Danny Hutton, Paul Barrère and Bill Payne. There are many others. These people make up a sizeable segment of the elite of a generation of American musicians. Between them they have recorded many great albums and sold many millions of records. George was crucially important to all of them. His opinion counted and his judgements were trusted. His approval was valued; his disapproval was the cause of reflection, self-criticism and re-evaluation.

It is hard to quantify a legacy like this, but it is a real legacy nonetheless, and George's membership of Little Feat is its most obvious expression. The albums he made with that band still sound unique a quarter of a century or more later. For a time in the mid 1970s critics were given to presenting George and Little Feat's commercial under-achievement as one of life's imponderables. How could a band this good have so much trouble selling records? Perhaps that question isn't so hard to answer. With no cohesive image, a wildly eclectic sound defying easy categorisation, and a fat lead singer with the dress sense of a baker or a mechanic, Little Feat were a marketing department's nightmare. But at their best, they had a skip in their step that made contemporaries seem dull and plodding. And they were at their best when George was fully engaged.

THE SEQUESTERED ARTISTE

For all his achievements with Little Feat, maybe George should have left the band sooner. The inability to resolve band tensions drained him, and in the last years the quality of his work declined. So many of those tensions came from his desire both to collaborate and to control. The obvious way for George to have resolved this conflict would have been to go it alone sooner, to work as a solo artist and only to call in collaborators on his own terms. As Ira Ingber says, "The sequestered artiste was very much a dominant part of his personality."[10] Operating as a maverick figure would have suited George, working on varied projects that took his fancy in the manner of people like Van Dyke Parks, Robbie Robertson and John Cale. But it didn't happen.

Because he could be so controlling George was often difficult to work with, although his enthusiasm for other musicians' work was genuine. Most of the artists mentioned in this book can tell of frustrations, fallings-out and breakdowns in communication with George. But for all that, he is spoken of with real warmth, affection and respect. As Hutton says, "He did have a wonderful spark about him."[11] Despite the sadness of his departure, and all the things left unsaid and undone, he is remembered with a smile.

George's genius was in his ability to do lots of things well. To sing, write, play and produce well. And he was an innovator – not by bringing obviously radical avant-garde elements into rock music in the way that The Velvet Underground or Jimi Hendrix had done, but by combining established and traditional forms in imaginative ways. Because he was working with mostly traditional and mainstream forms, the extent of this innovation has often passed unnoticed. And, conversely, it was because he was using traditional forms in an unusual way that his music has not reached a bigger audience. He occupied a perpetually uncomfortable position – too strange to be wholly accepted into the mainstream, yet not overtly experimental enough to be thought of as alternative.

George's odyssey through 1960s and 1970s American music is typical in many ways. There is the garage-band apprenticeship, the struggle to get established, the chart success, the many sessions, and the decline. But it is a unique journey because he was a unique talent. The drugs may have taken their toll and the extravagant gifts may have been dissipated. Too much energy may have been wasted on trying to hold together a band he could no longer control. Yet despite all of that, when George hit his stride he had that something that marks out great rock'n'roll music. Whatever you call it – feel, attitude, style – Lowell George had it. When he was at his best he had a strong sense of what felt right in a song, as well as the bloody-minded determination to keep chasing it. Unusually, he was able to combine this with both analytical intelligence and laconic humour. It was a rare combination of gifts.

CHAPTER 11

Lowell George on Record

"In the studio I hem and haw and waste a little time ... and then I just let it happen."

LOWELL GEORGE

Over the following pages we've compiled listings of the records that Lowell George was involved with. The first section (pages 150 to 155) covers the albums he made as a solo artist as well as with three bands: The Factory, The Mothers Of Invention, and, of course, Little Feat. Second (p156) is a selection of the singles he released with Little Feat and as a solo act. The third section (pages 157 to 167) details the work undertaken by George as a producer and session musician, with a commentary on individual records and, where known, notes on George's precise involvement. Finally (on pages 168 and 169) there is a chronological compendium of all the albums, providing a concise view of Lowell George's recorded legacy. The index at the back of the book will often point you to more information about some of the songs, artists and records listed.

Lowell and makeshift mobile rig

Selected Discography
ALBUMS

THE FACTORY

Lowell George & The Factory *Lightning-Road Man* (Bizarre/Straight Records R271563; 1993).
Largely a compilation of obscure singles and previously unreleased demos by George's first band, The Factory.

FRANK ZAPPA & THE MOTHERS OF INVENTION

The Mothers Of Invention *Burnt Weeny Sandwich* (US Bizarre RS6370; UK Reprise RSLP6370; March 1970)

The Mothers Of Invention *Weasels Ripped My Flesh* (US Bizarre RS2028; UK Reprise RSLP2028; September 1970)

Frank Zappa *You Can't Do That On Stage Anymore Vol 1* (US Barking Pumpkin D174213; UK Zappa CDDZAP8; 1988)

Frank Zappa *You Can't Do That On Stage Anymore Vol 4* (Zappa CDZAPPA40; 1991)

Frank Zappa *You Can't Do That On Stage Anymore Vol 5* (Zappa CDDZAPP46; 1992)

George's appearances on Zappa and Mothers Of Invention albums are the subject of some dispute. Most authorities think he appeared on *Burnt Weeny Sandwich*. He definitely contributes to one song on *Weasels Ripped My Flesh* ('Didja Get Any Onya?'), and possibly others.

The *You Can't Do That On Stage Anymore* series collects an enormous range of Zappa and Mothers material recorded over a 20-year period. Each volume is carefully annotated, so George's contributions can be identified with certainty. It should be noted, however, that he always played a minor role in the Mothers, so this material does not reveal much of interest.

LITTLE FEAT

Little Feat

(US Warner Bros WS1890; UK Warner
Bros K46072)
Released: US January 1971, UK
January 1975
Highest chart position: None

RECORDING: *Producer:* Russ Titelman.
Engineers: Bob Kovach, Rudy Hill.
Studio: United Western Recorders,
Hollywood; Record Plant, LA. *Recorded:*
Mainly autumn 1970; 'Willin'' based on
George home demo from around early
1969; 'Truck Stop Girl' probably late
1969; 'Crack In Your Door' mid 1970.

TRACKS: 'Snakes On Everything' (Payne);
'Strawberry Flats' (Payne/George);
'Truck Stop Girl' (Payne/George); 'Brides
Of Jesus' (Payne/George); 'Willin''
(George); 'Hamburger Midnight'
(George/Estrada); 'Forty-Four Blues' /
'How Many More Times' (Burnett); 'Crack
In Your Door' (George); 'I've Been The
One' (George); 'Takin' My Time' (Payne);
'Crazy Captain Gunboat Willie'
(Payne/George).

Sailin' Shoes

(US Warner Bros BS2600; UK Warner
Bros K46156)
Released: US February 1972, UK
May 1972
Highest chart position: None

RECORDING: *Producer:* Ted Templeman.
Engineers: Donn Landee (also Eddie
Bracken 'Sailin' Shoes', Bob Hata
'Trouble'). *Studios:* Amigo, North
Hollywood; Sunset Sound, TTG/Sunset-
Highland, Sunwest (all Hollywood).
Recorded: April 1971 to late 1971
(possibly into early 1972).

TRACKS: 'Easy To Slip' (George/Martin);
'Cold Cold Cold' (George); 'Trouble'
(George); 'Tripe Face Boogie'
(Payne/Hayward); 'Willin'' (George); 'A
Apolitical Blues' (George); 'Sailin' Shoes'
(George); 'Teenage Nervous Breakdown'
(George); 'Got No Shadow' (Payne);
'Cat Fever' (Payne); 'Texas Rose
Cafe' (George).

Dixie Chicken

(US Warner Bros BS2686; UK Warner
Bros K46200)
Released: US January 1973, UK
June 1973
Highest chart position: None

RECORDING: *Producer:* Lowell George.
Engineers: Robert Appere, Michael
Boshears. *Studio:* Clover Recorders,
Sunset Sound (both Hollywood); Amigo
(North Hollywood). *Recorded:* late 1972.

TRACKS: "Dixie Chicken'
(George/Martin); 'Two Trains' (George);
'Roll Um Easy' (George); 'On Your Way
Down' (A Toussaint); 'Kiss It Off'
(George); 'Fool Yourself' (Tackett);
'Walkin' All Night' (Payne/Barrère); 'Fat
Man In The Bathtub' (George); 'Juliette'
(George); 'Lafayette Railroad'
(Payne/George).

Feats Don't Fail Me Now

(US Warner Bros BS2784; UK Warner
Bros K56030)
Released: US August 1974, UK
September 1974
Highest chart position: US 36, UK none

RECORDING: *Producer:* Lowell George
('Spanish Moon' Van Dyke Parks).
Engineer: George Massenburg.
Studios: Blue Seas, Baltimore; Amigo,
North Hollywood; Sound Factory, Sunset
Sound (both Hollywood). *Recorded:*
January-March 1974 ('Spanish Moon'),
spring to June 1974 (all others).

TRACKS: 'Rock And Roll Doctor'
(George/Martin); 'Oh Atlanta' (Payne);
'Skin It Back' (Barrère); 'Down The Road'
(George); 'Spanish Moon' (George);
'Feats Don't Fail Me Now'
(Barrère/George/Martin); 'The Fan'
(Payne/George); 'Cold Cold Cold'/'Tripe
Face Boogie' (George, Payne/Hayward).

The Last Record Album

(US Warner Bros BS2884; UK Warner
Bros K56156)
Released: October 1975
Highest chart position: US 36, UK 36

RECORDING: *Producer:* Lowell George.
Engineer: George Massenburg. *Studio:*
Sound Factory, Hollywood. *Recorded:*
Between March and September 1975.

TRACKS: 'Romance Dance'
(Barrère/Payne/Gradney); 'All That You
Dream' (Barrère); 'Long Distance Love'
(George); 'Day Or Night' (Payne/Tate);
'One Love Stand'
(Barrère/Payne/Gradney); 'Down Below
The Borderline' (George); 'Somebody's
Leavin'' (Payne); 'Mercenary Territory'
(George/Hayward).

Time Loves A Hero

(US Warner Bros BS 3015; UK Warner
Bros K56349)
Released: US April 1977; UK May 1977
Highest chart position: US 34; UK 8

RECORDING: *Producer*: Ted Templeman.
Engineer: Donn Landee. *Studios*: Sunset
Sound, Western Recorders (both
Hollywood); Amigo, North Hollywood;
Record Plant, Sausalito. *Recorded*: Late
1976/early 1977.

TRACKS: 'Hi Roller' (Barrère); 'Time Loves
A Hero' (Payne/Barrère/Gradney);
'Rocket In My Pocket' (George); 'Day At
The Dog Races' (Barrère/Clayton/
Gradney/Payne/Hayward); 'Old Folks
Boogie' (Barrère/Gabriel Barrère); 'Red
Streamliner' (Payne/Fran Tate); 'New
Delhi Freight Train' (Terry Allen); 'Keepin'
Up With The Joneses' (George/Barrère);
'Missin' You' (Barrère).

Waiting For Columbus

(US Warner Bros BS3140, UK Warner
Bros K66075);
Released: February 1978
Highest chart position: US 18; UK 43

RECORDING: *Producer:* Lowell George.
Engineers: George Massenburg, Andy
Bloch, Warren Dewey. *Live locations:*
Rainbow Theatre, London, England;
Lisner Auditorium, Washington DC, US.
Recorded: Aug 2nd/3rd/4th 1977
(Rainbow); Aug 8th/9th/10th '77 (Lisner).

TRACKS: 'Join The Band' (no writers'
credits); 'Fat Man In The Bathtub'
(George); 'All That You Dream' (Barrère);
'Oh Atlanta' (Payne); 'Old Folks Boogie'
(Barrère/Barrère); 'Time Loves A Hero'
(Payne/Barrère/Gradney); 'Day Or Night'
(Payne/Tate); 'Mercenary Territory'
(George/Hayward/George); 'Spanish
Moon' (George); 'Dixie Chicken'
(George/Martin); 'Tripe Face Boogie'
(Payne/Hayward); 'Rocket In My Pocket'
(George); 'Willin'' (George); 'Don't
Bogart That Joint' (Ingber/Wagner); 'A
Apolitical Blues' (George); 'Sailin' Shoes'
(George); 'Feats Don't Fail Me Now'
(Barrère/George/Martin)
Rhino's 2002 CD issue has extra tracks.

Down On The Farm

(US Warner Bros HS3345; UK Warner
Bros K56667)
Released: November 1979
Highest chart position: US 29; UK 46

RECORDING: *Producer:* Lowell George
"with a little help from his friends".
Engineer: Ray Thompson. *Studios:*
Paramount Ranch, Agoura Hills; Lowell
George's home, Topanga (latter two
locations with Wally Heider mobile
truck); finished at Wally Heider
Recorders, Hollywood. *Recorded:*
Started late 1978; concluded August-
September 1979.

TRACKS: 'Down On The Farm'
(Barrère/Gabriel Barrère); 'Six Feet Of
Snow' (George/Keith Godchaux);
'Perfect Imperfection' (Barrère/Tom
Snow); 'Kokomo' (George); 'Be One Now'
(George/Fred Tackett); 'Straight From
The Heart' (Payne/George); 'Front Page
News' (Payne/George); 'Wake Up
Dreaming' (Payne/Fran Payne); 'Feel The
Groove' (Gordon Dewitty/Clayton).

Hoy-Hoy!

(US Warner Bros 2BSK3538; UK Warner Bros K66100)
Released: US July 1981, UK August 1981
Highest chart position: US 39, UK 76

RECORDING: Various producers, studios, recording locations, and dates.

TRACKS: 'Rocket In My Pocket' (George); 'Rock And Roll Doctor' (George/Martin); 'Skin It Back' (Barrère); 'Easy To Slip' (George/Martin); 'Red Streamliner' (Payne/Tate); 'Lonesome Whistle' (Williams/Davies); 'Front Page News' (Payne/George); 'The Fan' (George/Payne); 'Forty-Four Blues' (Burnett); 'Teenage Nervous Breakdown' [slow version] (George); 'Teenage Nervous Breakdown' [fast version] (George); 'Framed' (Lieber/Stroller); 'Strawberry Flats' (Payne/George); 'Gringo' (Payne); 'Over The Edge' (Barrère); 'Two Trains' (George); 'China White' (George); 'All That You Dream' (Barrère); 'Feats Don't Fail Me Now' (George/Martin/Barrère).

Hotcakes And Outtakes: 30 Years Of Little Feat

(Warner/Rhino R279912; 2000)
Four-CD box with one important CD of previously unreleased material, most featuring George in some capacity.

LOWELL GEORGE (SOLO)

Thanks I'll Eat It Here

(US Warner Bros BSK3194; UK Warner Bros K56487)
Released: US March 1979, UK April 1979
Highest chart position: US 71; UK 71

RECORDING: *Producer:* Lowell George. *Engineers*: George Massenburg, Donn Landee, Billy Youdleman, Ray Thompson. *Studios:* Sunset Sound Recorders, Hollywood. *Recorded:* 1976-1979.

TRACKS: 'What Do You Want The Girl To Do' (Toussaint); 'Honest Man' (George/Fred Tackett); 'Two Trains' (George); 'Can't Stand The Rain' (Bryant/Miller/Peebles); 'Cheek To Cheek' (George/V. Parks); 'Easy Money' (Rickie Lee Jones); '20 Million Things' (George/J. Levy); 'Find A River' (Tackett); 'Himmler's Ring' (Jimmy Webb).

SELECTED SINGLES

*An asterisk * means a difference to the corresponding album version.*

THE FACTORY
US singles

'When I Was An Apple'/'Smile, Let Your Life Begin' (UNI 55005; 1967)

'No Place I'd Rather Be'/'Smile, Let Your Life Begin' (UNI 55027; 1967)

LITTLE FEAT
US singles

'Strawberry Flats'/'Hamburger Midnight' (Warner Bros WB7431, September 1970)

'Easy To Slip'/'Cat Fever' (Warner Bros WB7553; January 1972)

'Dixie Chicken'/'Lafayette Railroad' (Warner Bros WB7689; March 1973)

'Oh Atlanta'/'Down The Road' (Warner Bros WBS8054, November 1974)

'Spanish Moon'*/Down The Road (Warner Bros WBS-8091, March 1975)

'Long Distance Love'/'Romance Dance' (Warner Bros WBS8174, January 1976)

'All That You Dream'*/'One Love Stand' (Warner Bros WBS8219, May 1976)

'Time Loves A Hero'/'Sailin' Shoes' (Warner Bros WBS8420, August 1977)

'Front Page News'* *was released twice as a single after George's death (WBS49169 January 80, WBS49801 August 81)*

UK singles

'Dixie Chicken'/'Oh Atlanta' (Warner Bros K16524, March 1975)

'Long Distance Love'/'Romance Dance' (Warner Bros K16689, February 1976)

'Time Loves A Hero'/'Rocket In My Pocket' (Warner Bros K16694, August 1977)

LOWELL GEORGE
US singles

'What Do You Want The Girl To Do'/ '20 Million Things' (Warner Bros WBS8847, May 1979)

UK singles

'Cheek To Cheek'/'Honest Man' (Warner Bros K17379, July 1979)

Sessions and Production

Chart positions indicate the highest position that the record achieved. The index at the back of the book will often reveal references to more information on the artists, songs and records listed here and throughout this section.

Mike Auldridge BLUES & BLUEGRASS
1974 (US Takoma D1041)
This album by dobro specialist Auldridge was recorded immediately before Little Feat made *Feats Don' t Fail Me Now*. It was an important session for George because it was the first time he had recorded with a bluegrass artist and the first time he met future Little Feat engineer/producer George Massenburg. George played slide guitar on at least one track, 'Everything Slides'.

Jackson Browne THE PRETENDER
1976 (US Asylum 7E1079, UK Asylum K53048); US chart: 5; UK chart: 26
Browne's note on the sleeve says: "Thanks to Lowell George and Valerie Carter for inspiration." Inspiration aside, George's contribution is limited to an appearance on one song, 'Your Bright

Baby Blues', a soulful, mid-paced number. He harmonises with Browne in the song's choruses, contributes a weeping slide solo, and joins in again with improvised slide licks over the fade.

John Cale PARIS 1919
1973 (US Reprise MS2131, UK Reprise K44239)
One of the best albums by the former Velvet Underground member. George plays acoustic guitar and slide guitar throughout, joined by fellow Feat members Bill Payne and Richie Hayward on keyboards and drums.

Valerie Carter JUST A STONE' S THROW AWAY
1977 (US CBS PC34155; UK CBS 81958)
Carter was formerly a member of Howdy Moon (see p160). In addition to recording with that group and as a solo artist, she has worked regularly as a backing singer for the likes of Jackson Browne and James Taylor since the early 1970s. This was her debut solo album, and the involvement of Herb Pedersen (see p163), Maurice White (of Earth Wind

& Fire), Linda Ronstadt and George give an indication of the funk, folk and country influences that permeate Carter's record.

George has four co-writing credits, 'Heartache' (George/Ulz), 'Face Of Appalachia' (George/Sebastian), 'Cowboy Angel' (Carter/George) and 'Back To Blue Some More' (Carter/George/Payne). He is also credited as co-producer on two songs, 'Cowboy Angel' and 'A Stone's Throw Away'.

The album was produced and engineered by Little Feat collaborator George Massenburg.

The Credibility Gap *A GREAT GIFT IDEA* 1974 (US Reprise 2154)

This was a comedy group that won fame with a satirical radio "news" show. Two members, Michael McKean and Harry Shearer, went on to star as guitarist David St Hubbins and bassist Derek Smalls in the 1984 spoof "rockumentary" *This Is Spinal Tap*.

Kathy Dalton *AMAZING* 1973 (US DiscReet MS2168; UK DiscReet K59202)

George and the rest of Little Feat backed Zappa protégé Dalton on this album, recorded in the lean period between *Dixie Chicken* and *Feats Don't Fail Me*

Now. Drummer Richie Hayward was particularly dismissive of the results, reputedly making his copy of the disc into a frisbee. Van Dyke Parks also contributes to the album.

Cheryl Dilcher *BLUE SAILOR* 1977 (Butterfly FLY003)

Dilcher was a rock singer, guitarist and songwriter active in the 1970s. Her three albums (also *Butterfly* and *Magic*) sold poorly and have yet to appear on CD. She now works as an actor in Los Angeles and continues to perform at small local venues. George played slide guitar on the title track, 'Blue Sailor'. Organist and guitarist Al Kooper, best known for his Dylan connections, is another notable name among the credits.

Yvonne Elliman *NIGHT FLIGHT* 1978 (US RSO RS13031; UK RSO 2394197)

Vocalist Elliman's big break came in 1969 when she was offered the role of Mary in *Jesus Christ Superstar*. She went on to appear in both the Broadway stage production and the 1973 movie version. She had several hits in the US and UK through the 1970s, and is known to millions for the song 'If I Can't Have You' from *Saturday Night Fever*. That song is included on *Night Flight*. George is listed as a guitarist in the general album credits, along with the MGs' Steve Cropper among others.

The Fraternity Of Man *GET IT ON*
1969 (US DOT 25955)
This was the second album by the group that Richie Hayward and Martin Kibbee joined after leaving The Factory. Bill Payne and George contribute to the record, made just as they were forming Little Feat. Van Dyke Parks also makes a contribution; his friendship with George began when they met at these sessions.

Tret Fure *TRET FURE*
1973 (US UNI 73141)
Fure's debut solo record was produced by George and recorded around the same time that she contributed backing vocals to Little Feat's *Dixie Chicken* album. Fure, who is still active, remembers George as an encouraging presence in the studio. George also called in his friend Bonnie Raitt to help out here.

The Grateful Dead
SHAKEDOWN STREET
1978 (US Arista AB4198; UK Arista ARTY159); US chart: 41
George was asked to produce this Dead album because the band felt he was qualified to provide an antidote to its over-produced predecessor, *Terrapin Station*. George did not complete the sessions. This was his biggest production job outside of Little Feat.

The GTOs *PERMANENT DAMAGE*
1969 (US Straight STS1059)
This oddity was George's first venture into production, an opportunity that came along through his association with Frank Zappa. The GTOs (Girls Together Outrageously) were famous groupies of the time. They were not, strictly speaking, musicians. The list of contributors includes members of The Jeff Beck Group; their presence and the Zappa connection afford the album the status of a collectable period piece.

John Hall *JOHN HALL*
1978 (US Asylum 6E117; UK Asylum K3075)
Guitarist and songwriter Hall was a member of Orleans, a band that recorded hit albums and singles in the early 1970s. This was Hall's debut solo record. He helped out George and Little Feat intermittently from 1975 when he appeared on *The Last Record Album*. Here George returns the favour with guitar and vocal contributions.

Chico Hamilton *CHICO THE MASTER*
1973 (US Stax ENS7501), 1992 (UK Stax CDSXE071)

Another record featuring most of Little Feat, and an indication of the versatility of George and the band who adapt their styles to complement the playing of jazz drummer and bandleader Hamilton. George later recalled that the album was assembled out of a selection of jams recorded over three days. The experience of working with Stax Records left him less than happy. He said, "We got paid for that work less than any other. They resold the product to an advertising agency and made a Porsche commercial out of it, and nobody got a penny for it. We even wrote the tunes, and nobody got any publishing money."[1]

Happy End *HAPPY END*
1973 (Japan URC URL1015)

Happy End were a four-piece Japanese pop band who intended to create "genuine Japanese pop rock". The line-up included bassist Harry Hosono, who later joined the more successful Yellow Magic Orchestra. Happy End coaxed Van Dyke Parks into producing this album, their third and last, when they turned up unannounced at the sessions for his *Discover America* album. George and the rest of Little Feat feature on the record,

with George's slide guitar especially prominent on 'Sayonara America Sayonara Nippon'.

Howdy Moon *HOWDY MOON*
1974 (A&M SP3628)

This was the group's sole album, produced by George except for 'Cook With Honey' (Michael Jackson – not the same one) and 'Lovelight' (Robert Appere). Appere had previously engineered Little Feat's *Dixie Chicken* album. George employed other members of Little Feat, as well as John Sebastian and Van Dyke Parks, to help out.

Howdy Moon were a three-piece folk-rock band with Valerie Carter (see p157), Jon Lind and Richard Hovey. According to Carter, "It was self-written, with really integral harmonies. It was very bizarre, quite honestly, and not that great, but pretty good considering we were teenagers, I guess."[2]

Etta James *COME A LITTLE CLOSER*
1974 (US Chess 60029), 1998 (UK Chess GCH8047)

The blues/soul singer travelled to the sessions for this album from a rehab clinic where she was being treated for addiction problems. George appears in the general credits for his guitar contribution. British writer Richard

Williams later praised George's work on this record, saying he echoed "the sulphurous eroticism of Etta James on her treatment of Randy Newman's 'Let's Burn Down The Cornfield'."[3]

Tom Jans *THE EYES OF AN ONLY CHILD*
1975 (US CBS PC33699)
Jans was an American singer-songwriter who recorded for A&M and CBS during the 1970s. He died in 1984. *Eyes Of An Only Child* is typical 1970s West Coast soft-rock, often reminiscent of The Eagles. George is credited as Executive Producer. He played acoustic guitar as well, and with Jans co-wrote the first song on the album, 'Gotta Move'. Little Feat are also represented by Sam Clayton, Bill Payne and Fred Tackett.

Barbara Keith *BARBARA KEITH*
1972 (US Reprise MS2087)
This is a strong album with country, folk and blues influences that was nonetheless overlooked by the public when it appeared. It includes one of Keith's compositions, 'Stone's Throw Away', which Valerie Carter later recorded for her first solo album (see p157). George is credited as playing guitar, featuring alongside distinguished names such as pianist Spooner Oldham and drummer Jim Keltner.

Linda Lewis *FATHOMS DEEP*
1973 (UK Raft 48501; US Reprise 2172)
Linda Lewis *NOT A LITTLE GIRL ANYMORE*
1975 (UK Arista ARTY109, US Arista AL4047); UK chart: 40
The British soul singer's career has ranged from appearing as an extra in *A Hard Days Night* to sessions with Frank Zappa and Elton John. Most of her solo records have sold poorly, although she did have one big British hit single with a version of 'It's In His Kiss' in 1975. George appeared on these two albums and is listed among the general credits in both cases.

Martin & Finley *DAZZLE 'EM WITH FOOTWORK*
1974 (US Motown M6797S1)
George gets a guitar credit on this obscure record, the only Motown album he is known to have played on. Drummer Jim Keltner also appeared, and The Four Seasons' Bob Gaudio produced.

Judy Mayhan *MOMENTS*
1970 (US Atco SD33-319)
Mayhan started her career in the early 1960s as a dulcimer-playing folk singer. *Moments* was her first album to feature electric instrumentation. It was an early session for George, and he plays guitar

and flute alongside Factory colleagues Warren Klein (sitar) and Richie Hayward (drums) who had both just left The Fraternity Of Man.

Kate & Anna McGarrigle *KATE & ANNA MCGARRIGLE*
1976 (US Warner Bros BS2862, UK 56218)
This was the debut album by the French-Canadian folk duo, co-produced by Warners staff producer Greg Prestopino, and Joe Boyd, best known for work with British "folk" acts such as Nick Drake and Fairport Convention. It contains the frequently covered song 'Heart Like A Wheel'. George appears on the album's opener, 'Kiss And Say Goodbye'. As one of four guitarists, his contribution is hard to decipher, but it doesn't sound like him playing the lead lines. His playing on the album's closing number, the traditional gospel song 'Travellin' On For Jesus', is of more significance. He plays an acoustic rhythm part throughout the song, and also adds evocative pedal-steel-style slide parts that are mixed very low.

The Meters *REJUVENATION*
1974 (US Reprise MS2200; UK Reprise K54027)
No musician credits are given on this Allen Toussaint-produced album, but George almost certainly contributed. The slide guitar interjections on 'Just Kissed My Baby' certainly sound like him – or at least someone who has managed to exactly replicate his style and sound. The album was recorded around the same time that both The Meters and George were working with Robert Palmer on his debut album (see opposite).

Maria Muldaur *WAITRESS IN A DONUT SHOP*
1974 (US Reprise MS2194; UK Reprise K54025)
Produced by Warners staffer Lenny Waronker and Joe Boyd (see McGarrigles, left), this was Muldaur's second solo album. George plays guitar on one song, 'Gringo En Mexico', for which he is given "special thanks" on the sleeve. The album also features the McGarrigles and Linda Ronstadt (see p164), both of whom George worked with shortly afterward.

Nilsson *SON OF SCHMILSSON*
1972 (US RCA LSP4717; UK RCA SF8297)
US chart: 12; UK chart: 41
Harry Nilsson *FLASH HARRY*
1980 (UK Mercury 63-02022)
Speaking to British magazine *Zigzag* in 1976, George said that when he wasn't

paid for his work on *Son Of Schmilsson* Van Dyke Parks suggested that he send a telegram to Nilsson with the message: "Pay me, schmay me." This George did – and the cheque arrived the next day.

Flash Harry appeared some years after Nilsson's commercial peak and is not a well known album. The second song is a version of the George/Parks/Kibbee collaboration 'Cheek To Cheek' that George had included on his solo album *Thanks I'll Eat It Here* a year earlier. George's name appears in the long list of musicians' credits, with an asterisk that leads to a note saying: "In memory." Bill Payne and Parks are also credited. This must have been one of George's last sessions before his death.

Robert Palmer SNEAKIN' SALLY THROUGH THE ALLEY
1973 (UK Island ILPS9294)
Robert Palmer PRESSURE DROP
1975 (UK Island ILPS9372)
Robert Palmer's debut solo album *Sneakin' Sally Through The Alley* was recorded in New Orleans with help from The Meters and George, who had just finished *Dixie Chicken*. He jumped at the chance when invited to record with Palmer and The Meters, both of whom he admired. The record opens with a cover of George's 'Sailin' Shoes'. (Palmer chose to add the missing g to make it 'Sailing Shoes', though the letter was still omitted from *Sneakin'* in the album's title.)

Most of Little Feat, including George, backed Palmer on his second solo record, *Pressure Drop*. It was made primarily at Blue Seas studio in Maryland, where Little Feat had recorded *Feats Don't Fail Me Now*.

Van Dyke Parks DISCOVER AMERICA
1972 (US Warner Bros BS2589)
The role that George played in Parks's second album was important, if hard to quantify. Parks says that George "was completely at liberty – in other words unemployed" at the time. "He brought great epiphany," recalls Parks, "as in the mock tango on 'FDR In Trinidad'."[4] The album includes a cover of 'Sailin' Shoes'.

Herb Pedersen SANDMAN
1977 (US Epic 34933)
George was delighted to be involved in this session with banjo specialist Pedersen, partly because it meant that he got to sing with Dolly Parton. She was a part of the "Howdy-Cracker Vocal Revue" along with George, Linda Ronstadt and others. They sing on 'If I Lose', to which George also contributes slide guitar.

Nolan Porter *NOLAN*

1971 (US Lizard A20102)

A rare soul record featuring all four members of the first line-up of Little Feat, *Nolan* is sometimes known under the title *No Apologies*. Mothers Of Invention drummer Jimmy Carl Black says he was asked if he would play drums on this album by producer Gabriel Meckler. Black in turn recommended George and Feat bassist Roy Estrada, and they introduced Bill Payne to play keyboards. Black did half of the album and then had to leave for other commitments, so Richie Hayward came in and played on the rest.[5]

Bonnie Raitt *TAKIN' MY TIME*

1973 (US Warner Bros BS2729; UK Warner Bros K46261); US chart: 87

There's an all-star line-up here including singer Taj Mahal and drummer Jim Keltner, as well as George, Bill Payne and Paul Barrère. The album includes songs by Jackson Browne and Randy Newman, among others. Raitt, speaking in the early 1980s, said: "*Takin' My Time* is one of my favourite records to listen to, although I started out with Lowell George producing it – and he and I got too close to be able to have any objectivity about it. That's the problem when you're a woman and you get involved with the people you work with – and I don't just mean romantically. It becomes too emotional. It's hard to have a strong woman telling the man her ideas when, in fact, the man wants to take over the situation. So that album had a lot of heartache in it. It was a difficult one to make, but now I like it."[6]

Randy Richards *RANDY RICHARDS*

1978 (US A&M SP4678)

Richards was better known as a television actor when he made this lightweight collection of undistinguished pop rock. George appears in the general musician credits.

Linda Ronstadt *PRISONER*

IN DISGUISE

1975 (US Asylum 7E1045; UK Asylum K53015); US chart: 4

George contributes a double-tracked slide guitar solo plus fills to Ronstadt's rather awkward country-rock interpretation of his 'Roll Um Easy', which is not an improvement on Little Feat's original.

John Sebastian *TARZANA KID*

1974 (US Reprise 2187; UK Reprise K54028)

One of George's best sessions was this little-known collaboration with ex-Lovin'

Spoonful leader Sebastian, whose career was then at a low commercial ebb. George co-wrote the poignant country-folk ballad 'Face Of Appalachia' with Sebastian, and also appeared on several of the album's other songs, including a cover of 'Dixie Chicken'.

Carly Simon *NO SECRETS*
1972 (US Elektra 75049; UK Elektra K42127); US chart: 1; UK chart: 3
Carly Simon *ANOTHER PASSENGER*
1976 (US Elektra/Asylum 106454-2; UK Elektra/Asylum 960609-2); US chart: 29
Simon's most famous hit 'You're So Vain' was included on *No Secrets*, which in turn was one of her biggest albums. George plays slide guitar on one song, 'Waited So Long', alongside Bill Payne on organ. According to the sleevenotes the record was recorded in Trident Studios in London in September and October 1972. Presumably some of the contributions, including those of George and Payne, were added in Los Angeles during the remixing stage, which took place at Sound Labs studio, because George's first visit to the UK is generally considered to have been for the Warner Bros package tour of early 1975. George helped out again on *Passenger*, drafted in by some-time Little Feat associate Ted Templeman who produced the album.

John David Souther *BLACK ROSE*
1976 (US Asylum SD5055; UK Asylum K53037)
John David ("JD") Souther was another regular on the Los Angeles soft-rock scene in the 1970s. He always seemed on the verge of matching the success of contemporaries like The Eagles but never quite managed it. George plays slide guitar on one song, 'Midnight Prowl', a moody, funky, mid-paced rocker. It is not one of his best session contributions but is notable because the song fades with George sharing an improvisation with noted jazz trumpeter Donald Byrd, who on this occasion is playing flugelhorn.

John Starling *LONG TIME GONE*
1980 (US Sugarhill SH3714)
George and one Audie Ashworth co-produced this album for guitarist/singer Starling. It was George's last production job outside Little Feat. He also contributes some brief trademark slide solos, and Emmylou Harris and Ricky Scaggs appear too.

James Taylor *GORILLA*
1975 (US Warner Bros 2866; UK Warner Bros K56137); US chart: 6
George plays guitar on one song, 'Angry Blues', where he and Valerie Carter also

sing harmonies. George said it was one of his favourite session appearances.

Mick Taylor MICK TAYLOR
1979 (UK CBS 82600; US CBS 35076)
The former Rolling Stones guitarist had made a guest appearance on Little Feat's *Waiting For Columbus* live record, playing on 'A Apolitical Blues'. George returned the favour, appearing on this, Taylor's first solo album.

Ivan Ulz IVAN THE ICE CREAM MAN
1970 (US Stanyan 10012)
A former jobbing songwriter and now a children's entertainer, Ulz recorded this very obscure folk/singer-songwriter album in 1970. He says, "I was under contract then to poet Rod McKuen as a songwriter and to make an album. I asked people I knew to come in and play. Jackson Browne did several tracks. Lowell and the Feat – except Richie, who was doing a session with Goldie Hawn – played on two of my songs, '1440 Broadway' and 'Grand Illusion'. Another drummer came in later and overdubbed drums. It was pretty awful! The album was, finally, a collection of rather awkward demos."[7] In fact, *Ivan The Ice Cream Man* has some pleasant songs in the style of early David Blue, but most of the arrangements do indeed seem

under-developed and the album as a whole sounds unfinished.

Various Artists PERFORMANCE SOUNDTRACK
1970 (US Warner Bros BS2554, UK Warner Bros K46075)
If one listens to this record divorced from its intended setting as a movie soundtrack, it seems a fractured, challenging album. Unlike many 1960s rock film soundtracks it is not a collection of pop tunes chosen to fit the theme of the film. Instead, producer Jack Nitzsche mixes orchestral and electronic textures with bluesy rock, proto-rap by The Last Poets, and rattling, twanging dulcimers and tablas, creating a selection of atmospheric mood pieces. Merry Clayton, sister of Little Feat percussionist Sam Clayton, contributes vocals. Other performers include Mick Jagger, Randy Newman and Buffy Sainte-Marie. George is not credited, but is widely rumoured to have contributed slide guitar to several songs.

Jimmy Webb EL MIRAGE
1977 (US Atlantic SD18218; UK Atlantic K50370)
The much-lauded songwriter became a recording artist for this George Martin-produced effort. Lowell George is listed

in the general credits ("electric slide guitar") along with just about every other Los Angeles session regular of the era. It's not obvious what song (or songs) he contributed to, but it could be him playing on future Feat member Fred Tackett's 'Dance To The Radio' – which is the only song on the album not written by Webb himself.

Bill Wyman *MONKEY GRIP*
1974 (UK Rolling Stones COC 59102; UK Rolling Stones COC79100); UK chart: 39
The presence of George on this first solo album from the artistically frustrated Stone must have felt like a triumph to Wyman. The Stones were known to admire George, and once approached Little Feat with an offer to join them on stage for a two-band jam – an offer George refused. But he agreed to appear on *Monkey Grip*.

Akiko Yano *JAPANESE GIRL*
1976 (Japan Philips S7001)
Japanese experimental pop singer Yano was 21 when in 1976 she recorded this debut album. George and the rest of Little Feat (apart from Payne) play on the five songs of the first side of the album, "the American side", while on the second Yano is accompanied by Japanese musicians. One of the

"American" songs, 'Kuma (Bear)', is notable for George's credits for guitar, flute ... and shakuhachi. The shakuhachi is a traditional Japanese flute-like instrument that he learned to play during the 1960s. On all other songs he is credited solely as a guitarist.

Discography by release date

1969

The Fraternity Of Man *Get It On*
The GTOs *Permanent Damage*

1970

Judy Mayhan *Moments*
The Mothers Of Invention *Burnt Weeny Sandwich*
The Mothers Of Invention *Weasels Ripped My Flesh*
Ivan Ulz *Ivan the Ice Cream Man*
Various Artists *Performance* soundtrack

1971

LITTLE FEAT *Little Feat*
Nolan Porter *Nolan*

1972

Barbara Keith *Barbara Keith*
LITTLE FEAT *Sailin' Shoes*

Nilsson *Son of Schmilsson*
Van Dyke Parks *Discover America*
Carly Simon *No Secrets*

1973

John Cale *Paris 1919*
Kathy Dalton *Amazing*
Tret Fure *Tret Fure*
Chico Hamilton *Chico The Master*
Happy End *Happy End*
Linda Lewis *Fathoms Deep*
LITTLE FEAT *Dixie Chicken*
Robert Palmer *Sneakin' Sally Through The Alley*
Bonnie Raitt *Takin' My Time*

1974

Mike Auldridge *Blues & Bluegrass*
Credibility Gap *A Great Gift Idea*
Howdy Moon *Howdy Moon*
Etta James *Come A Little Closer*
LITTLE FEAT *Feats Don't Fail Me Now*
Martin & Finley *Dazzle 'Em With Footwork*

The Meters *Rejuvenation*
Maria Muldaur *Waitress In A Donut Shop*
John Sebastian *Tarzana Kid*
Bill Wyman *Monkey Grip*

1975

Tom Jans *The Eyes Of An Only Child*
Linda Lewis *Not A Little Girl Anymore*
LITTLE FEAT *The Last Record Album*
Robert Palmer *Pressure Drop*
Linda Ronstadt *Prisoner In Disguise*
James Taylor *Gorilla*

1976

Jackson Browne *The Pretender*
Kate & Anna McGarrigle *Kate & Anna McGarrigle*
Carly Simon *Another Passenger*
John David Souther *Black Rose*
Akiko Yano *Japanese Girl*

1977

Valerie Carter *Just A Stone's Throw Away*
Cheryl Dilcher *Blue Sailor*
LITTLE FEAT *Time Loves A Hero*

Herb Pedersen *Sandman*
Jimmy Webb *El Mirage*

1978

Yvonne Elliman *Night Flight*
The Grateful Dead *Shakedown Street*
John Hall *John Hall*
LITTLE FEAT *Waiting For Columbus*
Randy Richards *Randy Richards*

1979

LOWELL GEORGE *Thanks I'll Eat It Here*
LITTLE FEAT *Down On The Farm*
Mick Taylor *Mick Taylor*

1980

Harry Nilsson *Flash Harry*
John Starling *Long Time Gone*

1981

LITTLE FEAT *Hoy!-Hoy!*

Rock and Roll Doctor

Footnote references are arranged here by chapter.

Chapter 1: I Wish You Knew The Story, pages 6-11
1 Author's interview February 12th 2002
2 CD notes from Lowell George & The Factory *Lightning-Rod Man* (Bizarre/Straight 1993)
3 Author's interviews May-June 2002
4 Author's interview May 17th 2002
5 *Topanga Messenger* April 1979
6 Author's interviews May-June 2002
7 Author's interview May 17th 2002
8 Author's interview June 21st 2002
9 Author's interview May 17th 2002
10 *Rolling Stone* August 4th 1979

Chapter 2: The Lightning-Rod Man, pages 12-27
1 Author's interview June 21st 2002
2 Author's interview May 31st 2002
3 *Zigzag* March 1975 / *Melody Maker* July 10th 1976
4 CD booklet from *Hotcakes And Outtakes: 30 Years Of Little Feat* (Rhino 2000)
5 CD booklet from *Hotcakes And Outtakes: 30 Years Of Little Feat* (Rhino 2000)
6 *Zigzag* March 1975
7 *Zigzag* March 1975/September 1976
8 Author's interviews October 2001
9 Author's interviews October 2001
10 Author's interview May 17th 2002
11 Author's interviews October 2001
12 Unpublished material from interview for *Zigzag* by Andy Childs January 17th 1975
13 Author's interviews October 2001
14 Author's interviews October 2001
15 *Rolling Stone* April 6th 1968
16 Author's interviews January 2002
17 *Zigzag* March 1975
18 Author's interviews December 2001
19 Author's interviews January 2002
20 Richard Kostelanetz (ed) *The Frank Zappa Companion* (Omnibus 1997)
21 Richard Kostelanetz (ed) *The Frank Zappa Companion* (Omnibus 1997)
22 *Melody Maker* July 10th 1976
23 Author's interviews January 2002
24 Author's interviews January 2002
25 *Crawdaddy* November 1974
26 Unpublished material from interview for *Zigzag* by Andy Childs January 17th 1975
27 *Mojo* July 1994
28 *Melody Maker* June 10th 1976
29 Author's interviews January 2002

Chapter 3: I'm Willin', Oh I'm Willin', pages 28-43
1 Author's interview March 13th 2002
2 *Rolling Stone* August 2nd 1973
3 Author's interview March 13th 2002
4 Unpublished material from interview for *Zigzag* by Andy Childs January 17th 1975
5 Author's interviews January 2002
6 *Zigzag* September 1976
7 Author's interviews January 2002

8 *Rolling Stone* November 26th 1970
9 Author's interview February 13th 2002
10 Chris Gill *Guitar Legends* (Studio Editions 1995)
11 Author's interviews November-December 2001
12 *Guitar Player* August 1976
13 Donald Clarke (ed) *The Penguin Encyclopedia of Popular Music* (Penguin 1998)
14 Author's interview with Randy Newman's archivist, Gary Norris, July 3rd 2002
15 Author's interviews May-June 2002
16 Author's interview February 13th 2002
17 Author's interview February 13th 2002
18 Author's interview June 21st 2002
19 *Rolling Stone* November 26th 1970
20 *Rock* issue unknown 1971

Chapter 4: Put On Your Sailin' Shoes, pages 44-57
1 Author's interviews March-May 2002
2 CD booklet from *Hotcakes And Outtakes: 30 Years Of Little Feat* (Rhino 2000)
3 Author's interviews March-May 2002
4 *Rolling Stone* August 2nd 1973
5 Timothy White *Nearest Faraway Place* (Holt 1994)
6 *Rolling Stone* August 2nd 1973
7 Author's interviews March-May 2002
8 *Zigzag* September 1976
9 Author's interview June 21st 2002
10 *Rolling Stone* March 30th 1972
11 Jan Mark Wolkin & Bill Keenom *Michael Bloomfield* (Miller Freeman 2000)
12 Unpublished material from interview for *Zigzag* by Andy Childs January 17th 1975
13 Author's interviews May-June 2002
14 Author's interviews May 2002
15 Author's interview May 17th 2002
16 *Streetlife* December 13th/26th 1975
17 Unpublished material from interview for *Zigzag* by Andy Childs January 17th 1975

Chapter 5: In The Bathtub..., pages 58-73
1 Author's interviews March-June 2002
2 *Zigzag* March 1975
3 Author's interview February 13th 2002
4 Author's interview February 13th 2002
5 Author's interview March 13th 2002
6 Author's interviews March-June 2002
7 Author's interview February 13th 2002
8 *Sounds* August 13th 1977
9 *Streetlife* December 1975
10 *Rolling Stone* April 10th 1975
11 Author's interview February 12th 2002
12 Author's interview March 13th 2002
13 Author's interview February 12th 2002
14 Author's interview February 12th 2002
15 *Rolling Stone* March 12th 1973
16 *Rolling Stone* April 10th 1975
17 *Crawdaddy* November 1974

Chapter 6: The Sound Of Shuffling Feet, pages 74-89
1 Radio interview by Mary Turner on *Off The Record*, 98 WIYY, Baltimore, September 1984

2 Author's interview March 15th 2002
3 *Zigzag* August 1976
4 Author's interviews November-December 2001
5 Author's interviews November-December 2001
6 *Hi-Fi News & Record Review* September 1980
7 Author's interview February 13th 2002
8 Author's interviews January 2002
9 Author's interviews March-June 2002
10 Author's interviews November-December 2001
11 Author's interview March 15th 2002
12 Author's interviews November-December 2001
13 Author's interview March 15th 2002
14 1975 interview, *Virgin Rock Yearbook* 1981
15 Author's interview April 4th 2002
16 *Streetlife* December 13th-26th 1975
17 *Rolling Stone* October 24th 1974
18 Author's interview February 13th 2002
19 Author's interview March 13th 2002

Chapter 7: Help Wanted, But Not Enough, pages 90-103
1 *Zigzag* March 1975
2 *Melody Maker* January 25th 1975
3 *Rolling Stone* April 10th 1975
4 *Mojo* July 1994
5 Author's interviews January 2002
6 *Rolling Stone* January 29th 1976
7 *Melody Maker* November 8th 1975
8 *Streetlife* November 15th 1975
9 *Zigzag* August 1976
10 CD booklet from *Hotcakes And Outtakes: 30 Years Of Little Feat* (Rhino 2000)
11 *Streetlife* December 13th/26th 1975
12 CD booklet from *Hotcakes And Outtakes: 30 Years Of Little Feat* (Rhino 2000)
13 *New Musical Express* 11th June 1977
14 Unpublished material from interview for *Dark Star* by Geoff Gough May 20th 1977
15 Author's interview May 31st 2002
16 Unpublished material from interview for *Dark Star* by Geoff Gough May 20th 1977

Chapter 8: Only Time Will Tell, pages 104-119
1 www.james-taylor.com
2 *New Musical Express* May 14th 1977
3 *Zigzag* August 1976
4 *Sounds* August 13th 1977
5 *Featprints* 1996
6 *Rolling Stone* July 14th 1977
7 *Sounds* August 13th 1977
8 *Featprints* 1996
9 Author's interviews March-May 2002
10 *BAM* August 28th 1981
11 *Mojo* July 1994
12 Author's interview February 13th 2002
13 Author's interview February 12th 2002
14 Author's interview May 17th 2002
15 Author's interviews May-June 2002
16 Author's interviews March-May 2002
17 Bill Flanagan *Written In My Soul* (Contemporary 1987)
18 *Melody Maker* May 21st 1977
19 *Sounds* April 30th 1977
20 *New Musical Express* May 14th 1977
21 *Rolling Stone* June 30th 1977
22 Author's interviews March-May 2002
23 *New Musical Express* September 3rd 1977
24 Author's interview May 17th 2002
25 Author's interviews May-June 2002
26 Author's interviews March-May 2002
27 Author's interview May 17th 2002
28 *Melody Maker* February 18th 1978
29 *Sounds* February 18th 1978
30 *New Musical Express* February 18th 1978

Chapter 9: 20 Million Things To Do, pages 120-133
1 Rock Scully with David Dalton *Living With The Dead* (Abacus 1997)
2 *The Boston Globe* April 4th 1978
3 *The New Hampshire* October 3rd 1978
4 *Relix* 1986
5 *Rolling Stone* April 5th 1979
6 *Topanga Messenger* April 1979
7 Author's interview May 17th 2002
8 *Rolling Stone* April 5th 1979
9 Author's interview May 17th 2002
10 *The Boston Globe* June 21st 1979
11 *Topanga Messenger* April 1979
12 *Sounds* April 7th 1979
13 *New Musical Express* April 7th 1979
14 *Rolling Stone* April 5th 1979
15 Author's interviews December 2001
16 Author's interview May-June 2002
17 *The Boston Globe* June 21st 1979
18 *The New York Times* June (probably 18th) 1979
19 Bill Flanagan *Written In My Soul* (Contemporary 1987)
20 *Rolling Stone* August 9th 1979

Chapter 10: The Last Record Albums, pages 134-147
1 *Melody Maker* July 7th 1979
2 *The Boston Phoenix* July 10th 1979
3 *Rolling Stone* August 9th 1979
4 *Sounds* July 7th 1979
5 *Little Feat Radio Hour* show 36
6 *New Musical Express* November 24th 1979
7 Radio interview by Mary Turner on *Off The Record*, 98 WIYY, Baltimore, September 1984
8 *Rolling Stone* October 29th 1981
9 Author's interviews March 2002
10 Author's interview June 21st 2002
11 Author's interview February 12th 2002

Chapter 11: Lowell George On Record (Sessions/Production), pages 157-167
1 Interview on Australian Broadcasting Commission FM, 1978
2 www.james-taylor.com
3 *Melody Maker* July 7th 1979
4 Author's interviews March-May 2002
5 Author's interviews January 2002
6 *High Fidelity* June 1982
7 Author's interviews March 2002

Acknowledgements

THE AUTHOR would like to thank:
Mike Auldridge; Andy Babiuk; Paul Barrere; Tony Bacon; Jimmy Carl Black; Johnny Black; Mike Bryant; Chris Cafiero; Andy Childs; Byron Coley; Andy Davis; Eddi Fiegel; Tret Fure; Matt Gale; Elizabeth George; Forrest George; Inara George; Geoff Gough; Bryn Haworth; David Hindes; Catfish Hodge; Laurie Hutton; Danny Hutton; Ira Ingber; Billy James; Jay Kahn; Martin Kibbee; Bill Lantz; Rick Leaf; George Massenburg; Phil McMullen; Gary Norris; Nigel Osborne; Bill Payne; Van Dyke Parks; Greg Provost; Pat Price; Phil Richardson; John Sebastian; Phil Smee; Peter Standish; Alan Sweet; Larry Tamblyn; Charles Ulrich; Ivan Ulz; Richie Unterberger; David Walley; Chris Welch; Richard Williams. And Madeleine Brend and Georgia Brend.

THE PUBLISHER would like to thank:
Stephen Bishop, Rick Conrad (Warner Strategic Marketing), Paul Cooper, Duane Fukumoto (Hawaii State Library), Dave Gregory, Wayne Harada, Tuck Hersey, Doug Hinman, Allan Jones (Uncut), Mel Lambert, Julian Ridgway (Redferns), Jim Roberts, Charlie Springer, Bruce Wheeler.

BOOKS & MAGAZINES

We consulted the following books during research for *Rock And Roll Doctor*.
Tony Bacon *London Live* (Balafon/Miller Freeman 1999)
Jonathan Buckley & Orla Duane (eds) *Rock, The Rough Guide* (Rough Guides 1999)
John Cale & Victor Bockris *What's Welsh For Zen? The Autobiography of John Cale* (Bloomsbury 1999)
Donald Clarke (ed) *The Penguin Encyclopaedia Of Popular Music* (Penguin 1998)
Francis Davis *The History Of The Blues: The Roots, The Music, The People From Charlie Patton To Robert Cray* (Secker & Warburg 1995)
Bill Flanagan *Written In My Soul* (Contemporary 1986)
Paul Gambaccini, Tim Rice, Jonathan Rice *The Guinness Book Of British Hit Albums* (Guinness 1996)
Guinness Who's Who Of The Blues (Guinness 1995)
Barney Hoskyns *Waiting For The Sun: The Story Of The Los Angeles Music Scene* (Penguin 1996)
Terry Hounsome *Rock Record 7* (Record Researcher 1997)
Richard Kostelanetz (ed) *The Frank Zappa Companion* (Omnibus 1997)
Jan Mark Wolkin & Bill Keenom *Michael Bloomfield: If You Like These Blues* (Miller Freeman 2000)
Bud Scoppa *Little Feat Saga* essay in booklet for *Hotcakes & Outtakes* CD set (Warner/Rhino 2000)
Martin C Strong *The Great Rock Discography* (Mojo 2000)
Virgin Rock Yearbook 1981 (Virgin 1981)
Timothy White *The Nearest Faraway Place: Brian Wilson, The Beach Boys, & The Southern California Experience* (Henry Holt 1996)
Frank Zappa with Peter Occhiogrosso *The Real Frank Zappa Book* (Picador 1990)

We also consulted back issues of the following magazines, newspapers and periodicals: *BAM*; *Billboard*; *The Boston Globe*; *The Boston Phoenix*; *Crawdaddy*; *Featprints*; *For A Song*; *Guitar Player*; *Hi-Fi News & Record Review*; *The History Of Rock*; *Melody Maker*; *Mojo*; *The New Hampshire*; *New Musical Express*; *The New York Times*; *Record Collector*; *Record Hunter*; *Record Mirror*; *Relix*; *Rock Around The World* (WBCN); *Rolling Stone*; *Sound International*; *Sounds*; *Strange Things Are Happening*; *Streetlife*; *The Times* (London); *Topanga Messenger*; *Zigzag*.

PHOTOGRAPHS

The pictures used in this book came from the following sources (page number first). *Jacket front*: Fin Costello/Redfern's. *1*: Jan Menacker Brock (Charlie Springer Collection). *2*: Pictorial Press. *7, 13, 29, 45, 59, 105, 135*: Michael Ochs Archive/Redfern's. *75*: Charles Springer Collection. *91*: Tim Marshall (Bruce Wheeler Collection). *121*: Michael Putland. *149*: Chalkie Davies. *Jacket rear*: Rex Features. We've tried to contact the original photographers in all cases; if you think otherwise please contact the publisher.

LYRICS

All lyrics reproduced in this book are used with the permission of Elizabeth George and Naked Snake Music.

UPDATES?

If you have new information please contact the publisher by writing to Backbeat UK, 115J Cleveland Street, London W1T 6PU, or email us at lowell@backbeatuk.com

"Some contend that rock'n'roll is bad for the body and bad for the soul." Lowell George, 'Teenage Nervous Breakdown' 1972